PUBLISHER'S ACKNOWLEDGMENT

The publisher gratefully acknowledges the generous help of the Hershey Family Foundation in sponsoring the production of this book.

The
DHARMA
of
POETRY

How Poems Can Deepen Your Spiritual Practice
and Open You to Joy

John Brehm

Wisdom

Wisdom Publications
199 Elm Street
Somerville, MA 02144 USA
wisdomexperience.org

Library of Congress Cataloging-in-Publication Data
Names: Brehm, John, 1955– author.
Title: The dharma of poetry: how poems can deepen your spiritual practice and
    open you to joy / John Brehm.
Description: First. | Somerville: Wisdom Publications, 2021. |
    Includes bibliographical references.
Identifiers: LCCN 2020028105 (print) | LCCN 2020028106 (ebook) |
    ISBN 9781614297208 (paperback) | ISBN 9781614297345 (ebook)
Subjects: LCSH: Poetry—Religious aspects—Buddhism. | Buddhism and
    literature. | Poetics.
Classification: LCC PN1077 .B57 2021 (print) | LCC PN1077 (ebook) |
    DDC 808.1—dc23
LC record available at https://lccn.loc.gov/2020028105
LC ebook record available at https://lccn.loc.gov/2020028106

ISBN 978-1-61429-720-8   ebook ISBN 978-1-61429-734-5

24 23 22 21 20   5 4 3 2 1

Cover design by Jim Zaccaria. Interior design by Tim Holtz. Cover painting by Kevin Sloan.

Printed on acid-free paper that meets the guidelines for permanence and durability of the Production Guidelines for Book Longevity of the Council on Library Resources.

Printed in the United States of America.

Please visit www.fscus.org.

CONTENTS

INTRODUCTION

This is a book about poetry as a source of wisdom. It argues not that poems are or should be didactic or prophetic—or that poets be regarded as sages making grand pronouncements about the meaning of life—but that poems embody and implicitly endorse ways of being in the world that anyone engaged in spiritual practice, or anyone wanting to live a more mindful life, might want to emulate.

Here's an example of what I mean, a haiku by the great Japanese poet, Kobyashi Issa (1763–1828), translated by Robert Hass.

> I'm going to roll over,
> so please move,
>   cricket.

The poem, like many of Issa's, is charming in its simplicity, its childlike innocence. Didn't we all once talk to animals, large and small? The poem is nothing more—but also nothing less—than a gentle warning and request spoken by a person to a cricket. The poet is not telling us how to live or arguing for the virtue of non-harming. Instead Issa *demonstrates* an attitude toward life and a way of behaving whose ethical dimension is plain to see. Even insects deserve our respect, the poem seems to say, deserve to live out their lives and not be harmed simply for being in our way. It's important also to note that the poem is not addressed to *us* but to the cricket. And what is the significance of that? What are we to make of a man speaking to an insect? It suggests a friendliness and care that Issa extends to all beings, even the most "lowly" among us. Indeed, the poem may be seen as a subtle subversion of the hierarchy which we humans impose, always to our own benefit, on the world around us. It implies that we are not separate from or more important than the creatures with whom we share this life, that we can and should address them as equals, and that we can be mindful of their well-being as we move through the world.

All this in just three lines, and without ever making a direct assertion about how one should live. Such is the power of poetry.

If poetry models certain kinds of outward behaviors, it also embodies and elicits certain kinds of awareness. Poems arise out of moments of heightened awareness, and as such they have the power to heighten our own awareness as we read them. For to truly enter a poem requires mindful attention, an alertness, curiosity, and open-hearted responsiveness that is very much like the awareness we cultivate in meditation. And if we can drop our usual way of engaging a poem—worrying about what it means, getting stuck on lines or words we don't immediately understand and then feeling self-conscious or frustrated for not understanding; if we can instead simply notice and appreciate what the poem is doing, just as one brings bare attention to thoughts and sensations in meditation, then our experience of the poem can be quite rich and rewarding, even if we don't entirely "get it." Of course I'm speaking of poems of great power and depth, poems that feel lit from within, poems that somehow evoke what we already knew to be true without quite knowing how we knew.

The poems I'll be discussing all have this depth and power. I've drawn all but two of them from *The Poetry of Impermanence, Mindfulness, and Joy*, and in many ways *The Dharma of Poetry* can be read as a companion to that collection. I conceived of this book while gathering poems for the anthology, as I began to see more clearly how the Dharma shines through so many of my favorite poems, even those by poets who were not Buddhists or spiritual in any conventional sense, though I would argue that writing poetry is by its nature a spiritual activity. I began to see that poems can play a role in the Dharma world that they have largely ceased to play in our literary culture: as sources of wisdom and insight, and as exemplary models of how we might think, feel, imagine, live.

In *The Poetry of Impermanence, Mindfulness, and Joy* I suggested that the poems in the collection could be seen as spiritual friends, companions on the path. Here, I would like to take that suggestion a step further to show how these poems can be seen not just as spiritual friends but as spiritual teachers, as powerful conduits for the Dharma. Poetry has always been deeply interwoven with Buddhist thought and practice, beginning with the oldest scriptures in the Pali Canon. We have the *Dhammapada*, a collection of the Buddha's sayings in verse, dating to the third century BCE; the Ch'an poets Li Po and Tu Fu in eighth century China; the songs of the Tibetan monk Milarepa, from the twelfth century; the great Japanese haiku poets

Basho, Buson, and Issa, spanning the seventeenth, eighteenth, and nineteenth centuries; modern and contemporary American poets such as Kenneth Rexroth, Allen Ginsberg, Gary Snyder, and Jane Hirshfield; and scores of other poets influenced directly or indirectly by Buddhist thought. From the beginning, poetry has served as a vehicle for expressing the Dharma, and the Dharma has been a source of inspiration for poetry.

Poetry brings us into living contact with the Dharma, it shows how the Dharma flows through our human experience, as poets work with *the truth of things*, the fundamental conditions of existence, the way things really are. The poems I'll be exploring invite us to enter imaginatively into those situations and test out our own responses. How would we relate to the cricket? And how *will* we treat the other creatures we encounter after we read this poem? This is not an idle or rhetorical question. It is a spiritual question—and one we must take seriously if we are to see poems not as literary performances but as models for how we might live.

Poems have this power to fundamentally alter both our behavior and our awareness because they appeal not just to our intellects but to our emotions and imaginations and physical presence as well. Former U.S. Poet Laureate Dana Gioia writes:

> A poem doesn't communicate primarily through ideas. It expresses itself in sound, images, rhythms, and emotions. We experience poems holistically. They speak to us simultaneously through our minds, our hearts, our imaginations, and our physical bodies.

It is poetry's ability to engage our whole being that makes it such a valuable way of not only thinking about the Dharma but *experiencing* it.

In times of crisis, people turn to poetry, both reading and writing it, for consolation, connection, and a truth deeper than can be found in the daily news. Poet and scholar Philip Metres writes that: "The events of 9/11 occasioned a tremendous outpouring of poetry; people in New York taped poems on windows, wheatpasted them on posts, and shared them by hand. . . . People turned to poems when other forms failed to give shape to their feelings." W. H. Auden's great poem, "September 1, 1939," written on the occasion of Germany's invasion of Poland and with its prophetic line, "we must love one another or die," was reprinted in major newspapers across the country, emailed and posted thousands of times after the attack on 9/11. That crisis may seem distant, even as the wars it heralded continue—but it may be that we have now entered an era of permanent crisis, as the karma of our abuse of the planet catches up with us, as climate catastrophes occur with greater frequency and intensity, and as our political culture becomes more chaotic and divisive. These causes and conditions have contributed to the recent surge of interest in—and need for—both poetry and mindfulness practices.

Cultivating mindfulness may not seem the most effective response to the cascade of environmental, social, and political challenges we now face. But perhaps it is the most fundamental and necessary response. For without a revolution in consciousness, any external changes we make will be hollow and short-lived. If we hope to solve our current problems in a way that lets us go on living in the same manner that caused those problems, we will rightly fail. As Einstein said: "No problem can be solved from the same level of consciousness that created it." Technological and political fixes, no matter how ingenious, will inevitably fall short if they don't arise from a fundamental shift in our consciousness, in the way we understand ourselves and our interconnectedness with all life.

In the essays and meditations that follow, I hope to show how mindful reading of poetry can help bring about that fundamental shift by heightening our awareness, deepening our compassion, and helping us to see more clearly the truth of our ever more precarious human predicament.

Part
One

1

POETRY *as* SPIRITUAL PRACTICE

One way to bring poetry more deeply into our spiritual practice is to see poems as exemplary, as modeling ways of behaving and modes of awareness that we might wish to adopt as our own. We do this by asking not what poems mean but what they show, what ways of thinking, feeling, and acting they are explicitly or implicitly endorsing. The English Renaissance poet Sir Philip Sydney understood poetry in this way. He asserted the fundamental truth that witnessing virtuous actions in literature inspires us to act more virtuously ourselves. Writing of Virgil's epic poem *The Æneid,* Sydney asks: "Who reads Æneas carrying old Anchises [Æneas' father] on his back, that wishes not it were his fortune to perform so excellent an act?" Sydney's "A Defense of Poesie," published in 1595, is the first fully articulated poetics in English literature. So this notion that poems model behaviors and can serve as teachers—can "delight and teach," as Sydney put it—has been around for a long time. It's right at the beginning of our thinking about the role and purpose of poetry. It's also at the foundation of how humans have learned for millions of years. Before we had language, *all* learning was by example. You didn't explain how to throw a spear or build a fire or help an aged father, you demonstrated it. Of course seeing poems as exemplary is not the only way to approach poetry, and many great poems will not yield to this kind of reading, but it is one way, and a way that can deepen and support our spiritual practice and inspire us to act more mindfully in the world.

Poems can also model beneficent mind states—states of loving awareness and clear seeing, of non-harming and non-separation—that we may aspire to ourselves. Beyond whatever its ostensible subject might be, a poem is always also about the quality of awareness that produced it. Simply by presenting that quality of awareness, the poem implicitly recommends it to us. And when we make contact with these deeper mind states, our own awareness is enhanced. Elizabeth Bishop's poems, in particular, always inspire me to pay attention to the ways she pays attention and to bring the same kind of mindfulness to my reading of the poem as Bishop has brought to the writing of it. She also inspires me, as many other poets do, to look and listen more carefully as I move through the world, to wake up from my habitual self-focus and actually *see* the world in front of me.

By focusing on what they're showing us—what ways of being in the world they're recommending—we see that poems can serve as spiritual teachers and that the teachings they offer are both simple and profound: pay attention; walk through the world with reverence and wonder; look closely at extraordinary experiences and even more closely at "ordinary" ones; see the likeness in seemingly dissimilar things; delight in the world's impermanent delights; feel into the joys and sufferings of others; treat all beings with respect; love the earth and know that you are not separate from it; talk to animals, plants, rivers, mountains, trees; listen for what they say back to you. These are elemental truths, the kinds of truth a child could understand but which modern adults have been encouraged to forget. In the form of abstract imperatives, they may not move us very deeply. But to see them embodied and enacted in poems, given shape and texture in the richness of language, in sound and image, in the rhythm and voice of a poem, is an entirely different experience. If we feel into the poem with our whole heart, with the mind and imagination, with our bodily presence and our spirit, we may come to know these truths in a much deeper and more healing way. And such knowing may change us.

Witnessing and imaginatively participating in the boundary-dissolving experiences rendered in these poems prepares the ground for transformation. Such poems show us that it's possible to move from living as an isolated self trapped in a meaningless, insentient universe to finding our home again in a world that is shimmering, alive, intelligent, continuous with us and responsive to our loving awareness. Whether it's Issa asking a cricket to move before he rolls over, or Whitman bending down to kiss his "enemy," or Chuang Tzu knowing the joy of fishes through his own joy, or A. R. Ammons seeing himself in a weed that sees itself in him, these poems give us powerful reminders that we are not separate from the world. And this is the truth we most need to realize right now.

Buddhist environmental activist Joanna Macy writes:

> The crisis that threatens our planet . . . derives from a dysfunctional and pathological

notion of the self. It derives from a mistake about our place in the order of things. It is the delusion that the self is so separate and fragile that we must delineate and defend its boundaries; that it is so small and so needy that we must endlessly acquire and endlessly consume; and that as individuals, corporations, nation-states, or a species, we can be immune to what we do to other beings.

This belief that we are separate from the earth and superior to all other living things is the root cause of our suffering and the suffering we are inflicting on the planet. The poems we'll be exploring undermine that belief not by arguing against it but by showing how wondrous it feels when the illusion of separation falls away.

But to fully experience a boundary-dissolving moment in a poem, we must first dissolve the boundary that separates us from the poem itself. When we analyze and interpret a poem, when we put all our energies into "figuring it out," we separate ourselves from it. The poem becomes an object of study, a problem to be solved. Analyzing/interpreting poems has its place and its value, but reading this way keeps us at a distance. In a mindful or spiritual reading, what we want is to *enter* the poem, to live in the field of its imaginative energy for a time, to appreciate and *experience* it rather than *think about* it.

The truth of non-separation—the absolute reality that we are simply another manifestation of life, that our bodies include the whole earth, that consciousness is not produced in the human brain but woven into the fabric of the universe—is a truth we may need to encounter a thousand times before we begin to feel and believe and live it. But when we do experience this truth, even if only for a moment, it's exhilarating. Here's how the character of Celie, in Alice Walker's *The Color Purple*, describes such a moment:

> One day when I was sittin' there like a motherless child (which I was), it come to me that feeling of bein' a part of everything, not separate at all. I knew that if I cut a tree, my arm would bleed. And I laughed and cried and I run all around the house. I just knew what it was. In fact, when it happen, you can't miss it.

Many of the poems we'll be exploring in this book are about such transformative, boundary-dissolving moments. Entering them fully, noticing and appreciating as much as we can about them, experiencing them from the inside out, can deepen our spiritual practice and water the seeds of our own transformation.

2

The SACRED PAUSE
FROST, RYOKAN, WRIGHT

When we step back and examine the workings of the mind—not only the contents of thought but the process of thinking itself—what do we find? A relentless, self-generating stream of words, images, memories, stories; repetitive loops of worries, plans, regrets, desires. We also come to see that we are not controlling our thoughts, or even in any intentional way actually thinking them. They're just happening—and happening according to deeply grooved patterns. In *The Wise Heart,* Jack Kornfield writes:

> Just as the salivary glands secrete saliva, the mind secretes thoughts. The thoughts think themselves. This thought production is not bad, it's simply what minds do. A cartoon I once saw depicts a car on a long western desert highway. A roadside sign warns, "Your own tedious thoughts next 200 miles."

Meditation allows us both to observe our habits of mind and to experience moments of spaciousness—breaks in the incessant flow of thought, rest stops along that 200-mile stretch of highway. Poetry presents another powerful way to disrupt the habitual momentum of the mind, its automatic reactions and obsessive self-concerns.

To fully enter a poem, we must first stop and step away from the more immediate demands of life and engage in an imaginative activity that has no obvious practical value. More important, we must shift out of our everyday consciousness—the speedy mind wrapped in its self-centered stories and projections. Poets help us experience this stopping. Indeed, a poet may be defined as one who stops, one who is inclined by temperament and training to step out of the ongoing flow of experience and look at it, and to help us do the same.

Robert Frost's most famous poem is a perfect example of the beauty of stopping.

Stopping by Woods on a Snowy Evening

Whose woods these are I think I know.
His house is in the village, though.
He will not see me stopping here
To watch his woods fill up with snow.

My little horse must think it's queer
To stop without a farmhouse near
Between the woods and frozen lake
The darkest evening of the year.

He gives his harness bells a shake
To ask if there is some mistake.
The only other sound's the sweep
Of easy wind and downy flake.

The woods are lovely, dark and deep,
But I have promises to keep,
And miles to go before I sleep,
And miles to go before I sleep.

It's important to realize that the entire poem is predicated on the poet's decision to stop. No stopping, no poem. And that is the difference between the poet and the horse, who may be seen as representative of the force of habit, the unconscious instinct to do what it has always done. "My little horse must think it queer / To stop without a farmhouse near . . . He gives his harness bells a shake / To ask if there is some mistake." Likewise, for most of us, caught up in getting from one place to another, there is no compelling reason to step outside the flow of time and simply notice—enter into, recognize our oneness with—what's happening in the present moment: in this case, the woods filling up with snow, the sound of "easy wind and downy flake" inducing in the poet, and perhaps in us, a kind of reverent trance.

It's also worth pausing to consider the furtive nature of this moment. The traveler notes, with relief, perhaps, that the owner of the woods will not see him while he stops to watch the snow fall. There is a privacy and intimacy in his unobserved, secretive looking. Because if he *were* observed, it would be with puzzlement or suspicion. Like the horse, the owner of the woods would also think it odd for someone to stop and gaze at falling snow. Our cultural pragmatism cannot easily comprehend or justify the impulse to look intently at something for no "good reason" (with the exception of officially sanctioned beauty like sunsets, oceans, mountain vistas, etc.). Snow falling in lonely woods does not fall within the acceptable categories of things that warrant our full attention. Of course, we as readers do observe the poet. We look at him as he looks at the falling snow. We see the snow through his eyes and we also see his seeing, see him in the act of seeing. The poem thus gives us an example of how we might comport ourselves in a similar setting or situation. The poet's behavior both in the poem and in the writing of the poem makes an implicit argument, a lovely one, in favor of stopping and looking.

But why? What does this stopping by woods on "the darkest evening of the year," the winter solstice, give rise to? A moment of extraordinary depth and stillness, and a reminder that there is a world of beauty that exists independently of human will and purpose. Frost says: "The woods are lovely, dark and deep," and we feel the attraction the poet also felt, the desire to go into those woods, to slip the world of duties and destinations, escape the constriction of egoic self-concern, and merge with that depth and stillness. The poet does not give in, but his repeating of the line "And miles to go before I sleep" suggests the difficulty of resisting that lure. (Even the snowflakes are "downy"—falling down but also evoking feathery down comforters). We feel the pull of those woods even after the poem has ended, how wonderful it would be to drop everything and immerse ourselves in such quiet amplitude, in snow that blurs and blends all things in its whiteness—a physical enactment of the seamless nature of reality, which in our habitual way of seeing appears as a series of separate things. In a sense the poem itself *becomes* the woods, an imaginative space where we can experience a deep and healing self-forgetfulness. The question then is, how long can we stop and stay with the poem, the hushed world it places us in. Can we feel the sense of wonder and reverence the poet himself has felt? Can we carry that feeling with us into the demands and distractions of daily life? Can we allow ourselves simply to stop and look?

One of Japan's most beloved poets, Ryokan (1758–1831), lived the simple life of a hermit monk, which is itself a kind of sacred pause, a stepping out of the conventional flow of life. Known for his love of children and workmen, Ryokan embodied the "Great Fool" archetype, an eccentric, playfully subversive truth-teller unconcerned with what others thought of him. His poem "First Days of Spring" shows how stopping, allowing oneself to be stopped, can give rise to a moment of joyful communion.

> First days of Spring—the sky
> is bright blue, the sun huge and warm.
> Everything's turning green.
> Carrying my monk's bowl, I walk to the village
> to beg for my daily meal.
> The children spot me at the temple gate
> and happily crowd around,

dragging on my arms till I stop.
I put my bowl on a white rock,
hang my bag on a branch.
First we braid grasses and play tug-of-war,
then we take turns singing and keeping a
      kick-ball in the air:
I kick the ball and they sing, they kick and
      I sing.
Time is forgotten, the hours fly.
People passing by point at me and laugh:
"Why are you acting like such a fool?"
I nod my head and don't answer.
I could say something, but why?
Do you want to know what's in my heart?
From the beginning of time: just this!
      just this!

—translated from the Japanese
  by Stephen Mitchell

Here, it is the village children who stop the monk-poet on his round of alms-gathering, but he is *willing* to be stopped, as no doubt the children are aware. (I suspect his initial resistance is a little play-acting to make his capitulation more sweet). And unlike Frost's, Ryokan's stopping is public rather than private. He is not only observed but ridiculed. The people passing by, those who will *not* stop, laugh at him: "Why are you acting like such a fool?" Like the horse in "Stopping by Woods on a Snowy Evening" who thinks it "queer to stop without a farmhouse near," these passersby can't fathom why one would waste time playing with children. But Ryokan isn't *wasting* time, he's stepping *outside* it. "I kick the ball and they sing, they kick and I sing. / Time is forgotten, the hours fly." Rather than answering back to those who taunt him, Ryokan speaks to us with disarming openness: "Do you want to know what's in my heart? / From the beginning of time: just this! just this!" Just this present moment, just what life is giving us and asking of us right now, things just as they are—*this* is where the richness of life can be found.

And how wonderful that instead of arguing with the passersby, he writes a poem, for us. That, too, is a kind of stopping. Because what do we typically do when someone insults or disrespects us? We react, more often than not, in anger and defensiveness. The ego feels attacked, and the ancient structures in the brain that evolved to ensure our survival flood the body with chemicals designed to make us take action, to fight or flee. So we answer back, either out loud, or in our heads, where the argument may be replayed for hours, days, weeks, years. But there is another possibility, and that is to pause, to create a gap, a space between the stimulus of the insult and the response of anger. Ajahn Buddhadasa calls such pauses "temporary nirvana." We are released from the defilements of ignorance, greed, and hatred, and can rest in spacious awareness. Pausing is key to not getting caught in reaction. It allows for the possibility of a different, more generous response—in Ryokan's case, a poem which even after nearly three centuries still speaks to us with refreshing simplicity and directness. But we needn't write a poem to feel the benefits of such pausing. Simply *not doing* what our conditioning impels us to do is healing. And just to read the poem mindfully—with patience, curiosity, and full imaginative engagement—is to have stopped for a moment ourselves and entered the timeless experience the poem describes.

James Wright was strongly influenced by ancient Chinese and Japanese poets, and his poem "A Blessing" participates in the tradition of sudden insight which is a crucial feature of Zen poetry. "A Blessing" reveals the transcendent possibilities that arise

when we pause and give ourselves over to a moment
of boundary-dissolving connection.

A Blessing

Just off the highway to Rochester, Minnesota,
Twilight bounds softly forth on the grass.
And the eyes of those two Indian ponies
Darken with kindness.
They have come gladly out of the willows
To welcome my friend and me.
We step over the barbed wire into the pasture
Where they have been grazing all day, alone
They ripple tensely, they can hardly contain their
    happiness
That we have come.
They bow shyly as wet swans. They love each
    other.
There is no loneliness like theirs.
At home once more,
They begin munching the young tufts of spring
    in the darkness.
I would like to hold the slenderer one in my arms,
For she has walked over to me
And nuzzled my left hand.
She is black and white,

Her mane falls wild on her forehead,
And the light breeze moves me to caress her
    long ear
That is delicate as the skin over a girl's wrist.
Suddenly I realize
That if I stepped out of my body I would break
Into blossom.

Like Frost and Ryokan, Wright is on his way from one place to another, and like them he feels compelled to stop, to interrupt that forward momentum. When he and his friend step out of the car, they are greeted first by the twilight that "bounds softly forth on the grass," an image which evokes the luminous nature of the moment and the liminal space the travelers have entered: the transition between day and night where mystical experience most often occurs. The three long *o* sounds in "bounds softly forth" create a sense of buoyancy, of slowing down and opening. The horses also welcome them: "they can hardly contain their happiness / That we have come." Because the travelers have stopped and opened themselves in this way, the world responds through the loving presence of the horses. It is as if their stopping has called them forth. Then the poet and his friend step over the barbed wire fence, a transgression—they are literally trespassing—that initiates the movement toward the poem's ecstatic conclusion. That initial *stepping over* leads to the poem's final *stepping out* of the body. It's easy to treat the line—"We step over the barbed wire into the pasture"—as purely informational, but it enacts, literally and figuratively, the non-separation that the poem is ultimately about, the dissolution of the boundary between human and nonhuman, self and other, body and spirit. The poet is shedding the limitations of the egoic, self-centered way of being in the world.

Crossing that boundary and entering the field allows Wright to do more than look at the horses; he makes contact with one, caressing its "long ear / that is delicate as the skin over a girl's wrist." Because Wright has stopped, because he has made such loving contact with the horses, he has been brought to a moment of transformative insight: "Suddenly I realize / that if I stepped out of my body I would break / into blossom." What an astonishing thing to say! I've read this poem dozens of times over many years, and that final assertion, and the authority with which Wright makes it, still shocks me, the strangeness and absolute rightness of it. But what would it mean to step out of the body and break into blossom? It's interesting that Wright does not tell us—only that he knows that *if* he did step out of his body, he *would* break into blossom. It's the *knowing* that he realizes and enacts in the poem. He knows that he knows. Or as the Thai Forest master Ajahn Chah might say, he has become "the one who knows." He sees that being in a body that appears separate from all things is an illusion. Our capacity for boundary-dissolving experiences, like the one Wright describes, proves it. The breaking into blossom itself cannot be described, only approached through metaphor. It is a post-linguistic feeling, a state quite beyond the reach of words. And so Wright only points to it, extending it as a possibility for us. Such transcendence, the poem implies, is always available, that step is always there, waiting to be taken, but only if we stop our ongoing momentum and let the feeling of wonder, reverence, and loving awareness arise in us. We might also say that in the act of writing Wright has stepped out of his body and broken into the blossom of the poem—that he has dissolved the boundary between human and poem—which is itself an invitation for us to do the same, to enter the poem as Wright enters the pasture, to be there with him in that shimmering moment by the roadside on the way to Rochester, Minnesota.

This is the beauty and the magic of poems: they help us see and feel the beauty and magic of the world when we allow ourselves to hit pause on our habitual thoughts and behaviors. And when we enter poems fully, when we *experience* them rather than *think about* what they mean, they can release us from our sense of separateness and from the kind of obsessive self-concern that leads inevitably to suffering. In that way, great poems are needed now more than ever, as we grow more and more removed from natural processes—and from actual physical contact with the world—and as we identify more and more strongly with our thoughts, the relentless momentum and reactivity of the mind.

A great poem can stop that momentum for a moment and help us see that *any* moment, fully experienced, is a gateway out of the realm of time and change into timeless awareness.

Meditation: Walking/Stopping

Walking-and-stopping meditation is a practice designed to help us interrupt the habitual momentum of the mind and shift from being lost in thought—worrying, planning, regretting, wanting, etc.—to paying close attention to what's right in front of us.

Choose a place to walk, preferably in nature, though this meditation can also be done in a town or city, someplace where you feel safe enough so that don't have to be overly vigilant and where you won't feel too self-conscious about stopping and looking at things. Before you begin to walk, simply stand and feel how your feet make contact with the ground. Shift your weight from side to side, one foot to the other, and feel how your whole skeletal structure adjusts to this movement. Bring your attention to the flow of your breathing and notice whatever body sensations are present.

Begin to walk at a slow but not funereal pace, about half as fast as you usually walk. Meditation teacher Tara Brach says, "If I walk half as fast, I notice twice as much." Simply walk and look. Let your eye be drawn where it will, but hold an intention to notice the things you typically overlook, things that have a neutral feeling tone, that don't call forth any strong feeling, positive or negative: the intricacies of the bark and roots of trees, the qualities of dirt and rocks, shadows cast by bushes and ferns, spider webs lit by sunlight; or, if you're in a city or town, the lettering on street signs, bolts on fire hydrants, twigs on the sidewalk, etc.

As you walk, feel when something draws your attention, when something seems to call to you or feels especially vivid. When that happens, let yourself go toward that thing and stop. Give it your full attention. Simply notice what's there in as much detail as possible without adding any conceptual overlay. Don't ascribe meaning to what you see and don't tell a story about it: just look. Bring a quality of warmth and friendliness to your looking. Feel as though what you're looking at is aware of your gaze and appreciates the attention, as if it might be saying, "Ah, how wonderful to be noticed! No one ever really sees me the way you are seeing me." Notice the physical features of the object but see also if you can sense any energetic quality emanating from it. Notice the quality of the relationship you're having with it, how it feels to hold it in your awareness. Stay with the object as long as you're able to keep noticing and appreciating it. When you're ready to resume your walk, bow to your new friend (inwardly or outwardly) and thank it for being there.

Begin walking again and repeat this process when the next thing calls out to you. Do this as long as it holds your interest. Notice the effect this practice has on you. Perhaps a deeper sense of connection with the "ordinary" things of the world will arise, or a sense of calm affection, or the spaciousness, appreciation, and gratitude that comes from freely giving your attention to things typically overlooked. You may also notice the difference between walking and looking and stopping and looking, and between those moments of bright attention and our habitual way of being lost in thoughts.

You might want to practice stopping and looking throughout the day, even if only for a few moments. It's remarkable what we can see when we stop and turn the light of awareness on the things we take for granted.

As the ancient Japanese poet Old Shoju says: "Want meaningless Zen? / Just look—at anything!"

3

SEEING CLEARLY
BUSON

Yosa Buson (1716–1784) was a wonderful painter as well as one of Japan's greatest haiku poets, and this disarmingly simple haiku feels like a sketch, or a Zen painting, done with just a few brushstrokes.

> The old man
> cutting barley—
>   bent like a sickle.

> —translated from the Japanese by Robert Hass

The poem is animated by one of poetry's most essential perceptions: seeing the likeness between apparently dissimilar things—in this case, a man and his sickle—which is the basis for all metaphor. I can imagine Buson walking by a field and seeing this man harvesting barley, and the delight he must have felt when he realized that the man, bent through work and age, had taken on the shape of the very tool he was using. On the purely visual level, the poem is satisfying; it lets us share in Buson's moment of seeing, and shows us something, a striking similarity, we would not likely have noticed ourselves. In our habitual, self-focused mind-states, we walk by such scenes all the time (a man cutting barley would have been a common sight in 18th century Japan) and don't really see them.

Neuroscientists have shown that we actually take in very little visual information from our environment. Instead of seeing the world, the brain simply fills in what it expects to see based on past experience. In *How to Change Your Mind*, Michael Pollan suggests that by the time we are adults,

> the mind has gotten very good at observing and testing reality and developing confident predictions about it that optimize our investments of energy (mental and otherwise) and therefore our survival. So rather than starting from scratch to build a new perception from every batch of raw data delivered by the senses, the mind jumps to the most sensible conclusion based on past experience combined with a tiny sample of that data. Our

brains are prediction machines optimized by experience . . .

In other words, we see what we expect to see. We have to make a conscious effort to take in more than what our past experience conditions us to perceive. And that's where poetry can help.

Poems arise from, and invite us to participate in, acts of deliberate, careful attention. Buson's poem is both a reminder to slow down and look more closely and a demonstration of the result of his own mindful attention. And when we look more closely at the poem itself, we may see that beyond its visual representation, it suggests something about how what we do shapes us. There's a kind of physical karma here, a cause and effect relationship between the man's farm work and his bent back. The old man cutting barely is reaping, in more ways than one, what he has sown.

Just so, for all of us there is a karmic relationship between our habitual physical actions and our bodily condition, and between our habitual mind states and our spiritual condition. In the Dvedhavitakka Sutta, the Buddha describes how our minds are "bent" by our thinking: "Whatever a monk keeps pursuing with his thinking & pondering, that becomes the inclination of his awareness." Or as Ralph Waldo Emerson said: "A man becomes what he thinks about all day long."

Every thought, every posture, every gesture—every moment of consciousness—shapes us. Feeling deeply into that truth calls us to think and act with greater kindness and awareness.

4

ELIZABETH BISHOP
and the
ART *of* SELF-FORGETFULNESS

❧

I

One of the great joys of writing poetry, and of reading it, is that it can release us from our habitual self-concern. All truly great poems, even those that are most personal, both emerge from and can induce states of self-forgetfulness. The egoic mind, dominated as it is by fear and grasping, pushing away this and chasing after that, has no use for curiosity and connection, or for the kind of spaciousness and openness that is the ground from which poems arise. A poem written from a sense of personal grievance, or whose purpose is to shore up the poet's self-importance, no matter how technically brilliant, will give off an unmistakable whiff of ego. But a poem that comes from an experience of selfless inspiration invites us to enter a state of blessed self-forgetfulness as well.

We might think the purpose of poetry is to perform dazzling feats of language, or to express brilliant insights and powerful emotions, or to restore our sense of wonder, or to speak out against injustice, and it may be all of these things. But I would argue that a more fundamental purpose of poetry, and indeed of all art, is to open a secret passageway to the freedom and refreshment that lies just beyond our self-centeredness. Elizabeth Bishop, in a letter to her biographer, Anne Stevenson, said it this way: "What one seems to want in art, in experiencing it, is the same thing that is necessary for its creation, a self-forgetful, perfectly useless concentration." Bishop's assertion about what one wants in art also applies to meditation, where concentration is freed from any practical purpose and the self is forgotten, or seen through for the illusion that it is.

Bishop's own poems offer powerful instances of this "self-forgetful, perfectly useless concentration." Here is "A Cold Spring," from her second book, of the same title. This is not a Dharma poem in any obvious sense, but it is an extraordinary example of sustained mindfulness. Notice how much Bishop notices in the poem.

A Cold Spring

For Jane Dewey, Maryland
Nothing is so beautiful as spring. —Hopkins

A cold spring:
the violet was flawed on the lawn.
For two weeks or more the trees hesitated;
the little leaves waited,
carefully indicating their characteristics.
Finally a grave green dust
settled over your big and aimless hills.
One day, in a chill white blast of sunshine,
on the side of one a calf was born.
The mother stopped lowing
and took a long time eating the after-birth,
a wretched flag,
but the calf got up promptly
and seemed inclined to feel gay.

The next day
was much warmer.
Greenish-white dogwood infiltrated the wood,
each petal burned, apparently, by a cigarette-butt;
and the blurred redbud stood
beside it, motionless, but almost more
like movement than any placeable color.

Four deer practiced leaping over your fences.
The infant oak-leaves swung through the sober
    oak.
Song-sparrows were wound up for the summer,
and in the maple the complementary cardinal
cracked a whip, and the sleeper awoke,
stretching miles of green limbs from the south.
In his cap the lilacs whitened,
then one day they fell like snow.
Now, in the evening,
a new moon comes.
The hills grow softer. Tufts of long grass show
where each cow-flop lies.
The bull-frogs are sounding,
slack strings plucked by heavy thumbs.
Beneath the light, against your white front door,
the smallest moths, like Chinese fans,
flatten themselves, silver and silver-gilt
over pale yellow, orange, or gray.
Now, from the thick grass, the fireflies
begin to rise:
up, then down, then up again:
lit on the ascending flight,
drifting simultaneously to the same height,
—exactly like the bubbles in champagne.
—Later on they rise much higher.

And your shadowy pastures will be able to offer
these particular glowing tributes
every evening now throughout the summer.

Bishop once remarked that her favorite reading was Darwin, in large part because he was such a precise and dedicated observer of the natural world. Here, Bishop's own powers of observation, both panoramic and minute, are on full display. She captures the sweep of spring, the feeling of life renewing itself, through many vivid particulars: the violet "lawed on the lawn," a calf being born, deer practicing leaping over fences, the dogwood trees—"each petal burned, apparently, by a cigarette butt"—the lilacs whose blossoms "fall like snow," the song sparrows "wound up for summer," the "complementary cardinal," the bull-frogs, moths, and fireflies. She humanizes spring itself in a lovely metaphor, as the "sleeper" who awakes "stretching miles of green limbs from the south," reminding us of the bodily connection between the limbs of trees and our own limbs, the way we stretch our arms and legs when we wake from sleep. Spring calls forth an awakening from the sleep of dormancy, and to pay such loving attention to the stirrings of new life, as Bishop does here, is to awaken from the sleep of self-concern and the illusion of separation.

Bishop herself is nowhere in this poem, and everywhere. She is the witnessing presence that beholds everything, a field of awareness in which life is happening. She does not add her own personal story to this scene, nor does she interpret what she's seeing and hearing, or attempt to make any grand or summarizing statements about spring. The poem is, rather, a tribute to life and an expression of gratitude to her friend Jane Dewey, (the daughter of philosopher John Dewey), at whose farm Bishop enjoyed extended stays on several occasions.

What is most remarkable about this description is the way Bishop's own creative energies, her tremendous facility with metaphor in particular, reflect and amplify the creative energies of the earth itself. She doesn't simply *record* what she sees and hears as accurately and precisely as possible, as a naturalist might (though she valued precision and accuracy very highly); she casts her imagination over this landscape and fully *participates* in the fecundity of spring. A mind that can perceive that bull-frogs sound like "slack strings plucked by heavy thumbs" or that fireflies are "lit on the ascending flight, / drifting simultaneously to the same height, / — exactly like the bubbles in champagne" is fully alive to the connections and mirrorings that are hidden in plain sight all around us (just as the poem's many subtle and irregularly placed rhymes—*oak/awoke*, *champagne/again*, *fireflies/rise*, etc.—reflect the mirroring sounds of words). To make these connections, to fashion a new image out of two seemingly unconnected things, is the essence of the creative act, a linguistic equivalent of the union of opposites—male and female, earth and sky, form and formlessness—which gives birth to new life.

In a letter to Robert Lowell, Bishop wrote: "My passion for accuracy may strike you as old-maidish—but since we do float on an unknown sea I think we should examine the other floating things that come our way very carefully; who knows what might depend on it?" One of the things that depended on this passion for accuracy was her own well-being. Bishop had an extremely traumatic childhood. Her father died when she was just eight months old, and her mother never recovered from the shock of that loss. Mentally unstable throughout Bishop's early life, she had a psychotic break and had to be institutionalized when Bishop was five. Bishop never saw her mother again. She was raised by kind and loving maternal grandparents and aunts in Great Village, Nova Scotia, but was brought to Boston against her will—she described it as a kidnapping—to live with the more prosperous but emotionally distant paternal grandparents when she was eleven. Here she suffered neglect and abuse. One uncle dangled her over a second-story balcony by her hair; another sexually abused her. She would later describe them as "real sadists." Bishop was also severely asthmatic and was plagued by anxiety and depression throughout her life. In adulthood, she turned to alcohol to manage her pain, and her drinking nearly killed her. She felt deep shame about her inability to stay sober. She was also a lesbian at a time when it was unsafe to be so openly.

It seems clear now that her love of sustained and detailed observation provided some solace from her suffering. Focusing her attention on the things of the world, as she does in "A Cold Spring" and so many other poems, allowed her—we might even say *required* her—to forget herself, her painful personal history. Unlike the confessional poets of her era—Robert Lowell, Sylvia Plath, Anne Sexton, and others, who spoke openly about their most traumatic emotional experiences—Bishop was remarkably reticent about her own struggles and never refers to them directly in her poetry. Instead, writing poetry became, I believe, a kind of refuge for her, particularly in her more meditative, landscape poems. Which is not to say that her poems enact a repression of her emotional pain; they are a transmutation of it, the age-old poetic alchemy that turns sorrow into beauty.

Can such poems provide a refuge for us as well? I think they can. "A Cold Spring" is both an example of and an invitation to the joy of self-forgetfulness. It shows us what happens when we give our full attention to the world but leave our own story out of it. And if we bring the same kind of mindful noticing to the poem that Bishop has brought to the landscape she describes *in* the poem, we can enter the space of self-forgetfulness that Bishop has created for us. The small self, the grasping mind, will want to interpret or analyze the poem in order to bring it under control, pin it down, make it mean one thing that can be clearly summarized, argued for, defended. This is what the small self does: it tries to reduce wide open reality to manageable bits in order to soothe its own anxiety in the face of the mystery and ultimate unknowability of life. But what happens if we just immerse ourselves in the poem, if we simply notice what Bishop notices, delight in what she delights in, feel the incredible aliveness that is both in the landscape she describes and in the language she uses to describe it? Then we, too, might experience a moment of self-forgetfulness, free from grasping and aversion, at peace with things as they are, simply aware of what is.

II

Bishop was responsive not only to the beauty of the world but also to the kind of "ordinary," un-beautiful scene that we typically ignore. Here are the first five stanzas of "Filling Station."

Filling Station

Oh, but it is dirty!
—this little filling station,
oil-soaked, oil-permeated
to a disturbing, over-all
black translucency.
Be careful with that match!

Father wears a dirty,
oil-soaked monkey suit
that cuts him under the arms,
and several quick and saucy

and greasy sons assist him
(it's a family filling station),
all quite thoroughly dirty.

Do they live in the station?
It has a cement porch
behind the pumps, and on it
a set of crushed and grease-
impregnated wickerwork;
on the wicker sofa
a dirty dog, quite comfy.

Some comic books provide
the only note of color—
of certain color. They lie
upon a big dim doily
draping a taboret
(part of the set), beside
a big hirsute begonia.

Why the extraneous plant?
Why the taboret?
Why, oh why, the doily?
(Embroidered in daisy stitch
with marguerites, I think,
and heavy with gray crochet.)

Bishop brings a mindful noticing to a place most of us would consider unworthy of our attention, if we considered it at all. But attend to it she does, noting not only that father's uniform is dirty but that it "cuts him under the arms," that the wickerwork is crushed and saturated with grease, that the dirty dog is "quite comfy," that the begonia is hairy, that some comic books provide the only "note of color— / of certain color" in the "overall black translucency" of the filling station. But when Bishop notices unlikely touches of beauty, it sparks her curiosity: "Do they live in the station?" "Why the extraneous plant? / Why the taboret? / Why, oh why, the doily?" (She even notices the detailed stitching on the doily; the attentive reader might in turn notice that "doily" contains the word "oily,"— an instance of Bishop's subtle wit). It is this curiosity that leads to the transcendent revelation in the poem's final stanza, the awareness that:

Somebody embroidered the doily.
Somebody waters the plant,
or oils it, maybe. Somebody
arranges the rows of cans
so that they softly say:
ESSO—SO—SO—SO

to high-strung automobiles.
Somebody loves us all.

The poem leaves open who that somebody is, but as Bishop says, "it's a family filling station," so we can reasonably assume it's the mother who has added these domestic touches. But in a larger sense Bishop may be pointing to the human impulse to beautify, an impulse that occurs in all cultures and extends back to Paleolithic cave paintings in France and Spain. The arrangement of rows of Esso oil cans "so that they softly say / ESSO—SO—SO—SO / to high-strung automobiles," is a poem in miniature, a surprising and pleasing arrangement of words that has, in this case, a soothing effect on "high-strung automobiles," their high-strung drivers, and perhaps on us as well. It is also an example of taking an object with a clear practical purpose, a can of oil, and aestheticizing it, so that its artistic function outstrips its practical one, a momentary triumph of beauty over utility. The final line of the poem extends the care that has gone into these flourishes to everyone: "Somebody loves us all." We might recall here that Bishop lost her own mother at a very young age. Moments like the one she describes in "Filling Station," moments when one senses that the universe is suffused with a loving presence, where beauty can be found even in the most unlikely places, would have been especially powerful and healing for her. But such moments, and even the representations of such moments in poems, can be healing for all of us.

I've perhaps been making the poem seem terribly serious, but we shouldn't overlook its playfulness. Lines like "And several quick and saucy / and greasy sons assist him," with all those slippery *s* sounds, and the humor of "Somebody waters the plant, / or oils it, maybe" contribute to the poem's lighthearted tone. Some critics have argued that the poem expresses an elitist condescension toward ordinary working people, and that Bishop, who had a trust fund that afforded her basic financial security, is making fun of these people. But attention is a form of affection—Sharon Salzberg says "to pay attention is to love"—and the fact that Bishop looks so closely and carefully at this filling station, and at the father and sons who work there, makes the poem feel appreciative rather than dismissive.

Like "A Cold Spring," "Filling Station" is a celebratory poem, a poem that revels in the joy of simply looking, and dissolves the sense of separation between observer and observed. And like the mother who has tried to add some softness and beauty to the filling station, Bishop sees the possibilities for beauty in this "thoroughly dirty" place; she collaborates with the mother by writing a poem that is itself quite lovely. The mother's efforts, very likely lost on the men in the station, are not lost on Bishop, nor on us. In this way, the poem completes the transformation that the mother began. Or perhaps it would be more true to say that in noticing and appreciating what Bishop has noticed and appreciated, we as readers complete the transformation, and that within the space of the poem, the filling station has been emptied of its practical purpose, supplying gasoline to automobiles, and instead now serves to fill the reader with a sense of wonder, of being cared for by an unseen presence: "Somebody loves us all."

The great thirteenth-century Zen master Dogen said: "To forget the self is to be enlightened by all things." As Bishop's poems make clear, one way to forget the self is to enlarge our capacity for mindful, warm-hearted attention. Her poems are filled with the depth and richness that comes when we bring such attention to the present moment, the closeness and connection that arises when we embrace the things of this world freely and without reference to our own self-centered stories and desires. In that sense, "A Cold Spring" and "Filling Station" embody and implicitly promote a way of being in the world: open, curious, attentive, able to forget the self and to remember the aliveness in all things, however magical or ordinary (or both) they might be.

Meditation: Space and Timeless Awareness

This walking meditation is designed to heighten our awareness of awareness and of the relationship between awareness, time, and space.

We say that awareness is timeless because it has no features, no form, that could be subject to time and therefore change. It is empty, immaterial. In this way it is much like space. Space, too, has no features, no form, nothing that could suffer the effects of time and change. The contents of awareness—our thoughts, sensations, feelings, etc.—are constantly changing, but the awareness that regards them is always the same. Just so, the contents of space are constantly changing. Think of a meditation hall: people arrive and leave, sit and walk; chairs and cushions are brought out and put away; but the space in which these changes are happening—not the air but the space—remains unchanged.

In this meditation, which derives from Eckhart Tolle's teachings, we practice noticing the space between and around everything. Just as we are conditioned to focus on our thoughts, rather than the space between thoughts, we are conditioned to focus on objects rather than the space between them. Shifting the focus of our outward visual attention from things to space can help us detach from thoughts and relax into awareness itself.

This practice can be done anywhere, in a city or out in nature, where you can walk with minimal interruption and with enough of a sense of safety that you don't have to scan the environment for dangers. It helps to walk in a place where the visual environment is not too crowded, but I have enjoyed this walking meditation in New York City, so it can be done.

Before you begin, simply stand and feel the contact your feet make with the ground. You might sway a little and feel your skeleton moving, all the micro-adjustments your skeletal structure has to make to keep you upright. Begin walking slowly, at a pace that feels right to you. As you walk practice shifting your attention from objects in space to space itself. If you're walking in nature, notice the space between trees, the space between rocks, between bushes, between one branch and another, one leaf and another, etc. If you're in a city, notice the space between houses or buildings, the space between one parked car and another, between streetlights, between fence railings, between telephone poles. There's space between *everything*. You just have to look for space. If you're indoors, notice the space between objects in a room, the space between floor and ceiling, between walls, the space that surrounds a lamp, the space between chair legs, table legs, between sofa and chairs.

It's important to remember that the entire visual field need not be empty for you to look at the space between things. That is, when you look at the space between two trees and can see more tress in the distance that seem to fill that visual space, the space *directly between the trees* is still empty.

Practice moving your attention back and forth between objects and space—but give most of your attention to space. Let yourself stare at space, at what is *not* there. Without thinking about what it means, simply notice how this *feels*. Perhaps you'll sense a quality of shimmering in empty space, a stillness and aliveness; that outer stillness may correspond to an inner stillness and spaciousness that you're now able to feel more fully in yourself. Or maybe some other feeling will arise. Whatever it is, just allow it to be there and let yourself be curious about it. You'll get a clearer sense of the different feeling states that arise with perception of objects and perception of space as you pendulate back and forth between them.

Perhaps you'll feel refreshed after this walking meditation. And if you can practice sitting right after walking, you may experience more space between each thought, sensation, or feeling.

This practice of awareness of space can be done briefly throughout the day simply by taking a moment to withdraw our attention from objects and notice the space around them.

5

INTIMATE
ATTENTION
Saigyo

❧

As a young man in twelfth-century Kyoto, Saigyo was a member of the emperor's palace guard, skilled in horsemanship, archery, and other martial arts. But he abruptly left the court for reasons that remain mysterious—he may have had a scandalous affair with a woman of higher social rank—and became a wandering monk. He spent his days roaming the Yoshino mountains, meditating, composing poems, and admiring cherry blossoms.

> "Detached" observer
> of blossoms finds himself in time
> intimate with them—
> so, when they separate from the branch,
> it's he who falls . . . deeply into grief.

> —translated from the Japanese by William LeFleur

Here he describes himself as a "detached" observer of blossoms, the quotation marks in the translation indicating an ironic distancing from the concept of detachment. Saigyo may be playing on the (mistaken) notion that the goal of Buddhist practice is to become "detached" from any emotional investment in the world, to become cool and indifferent—a common misconception about Buddhism, prevalent, apparently, even in Saigyo's Japan.

Saigyo is clearly *not* detached in that sense. (Though he *is* detached from the self, referring to himself not as "I" but simply as an "observer of blossoms"). That observer "finds himself in time / intimate with them—". "Finds himself in time" is a resonant phrase, which can be read as "finds himself after some time" or as "finding himself in the world of time and change . . ." It is this awareness of impermanence that gives rise to his intimacy with blossoms. Because they exist in time, he knows they're going to fall, knows they're going to "separate"—become detached—from the branch, and that makes their beauty all the more poignant. And because he is not separate from them, when they do fall from the branch, "it's he who falls . . . deeply into grief." The poet is so deeply intertwined with the cherry blossoms that he becomes them—or rather, the illusion of separation is dissolved—and he feels himself falling as they fall.

The experience described in the poem may have been colored by the separation Saigyo had suffered as a young man when he left the highly organized structure of court life for the solitude of a wondering monk. Many of his poems deal with loneliness and nostalgia. But however much the poem may reflect Saigyo's personal history, it points to a larger truth. It suggests that when we become truly intimate with the things of the world, when we give them our loving attention and realize we are not separate from them, we make ourselves vulnerable to the pain of their passing, but we also get to fully experience their beauty. And this is what is being asked of us, always and especially right now: that we wake up from the dream of separation and love the world wholeheartedly.

6

LISTENING
William Stafford AND *Denise Levertov*

Poetry both arises from and invites states of deep listening. A poet must attune their ear both to the voice of their imagination, where the poem originates, and to the sounds of their material, language, where the poem manifests. So, too, when we read a poem, we listen both to the speaker's voice, as it shapes itself in words, and to our inner response to that voice, the way the poem resonates inside us. And when a poem is explicitly *about* the act of listening, we have another layer to attend to: our awareness of the poet's awareness.

William Stafford's "Listening" and Denise Levertov's "Aware" give us two vivid examples of mindful listening, and two invitations to practice deeper listening ourselves.

Listening

My father could hear a little animal step,
or a moth in the dark against the screen,
and every far sound called the listening out
into places where the rest of us had never been.

More spoke to him from the soft wild night
than came to our porch for us on the wind;
we would watch him look up and his face go keen
till the walls of the world flared, widened.

My father heard so much that we still stand
inviting the quiet by turning the face,
waiting for a time when something in the night
will touch us too from that other place.

In Stafford's poem, the father displays an extraor-
dinary quality of attention. Attuned to sounds both
near and far, he can hear "a little animal step / or
a moth in the dark against the screen." But he is
also a kind of sonic explorer, listening into places
beyond the auditory reach of the rest of the family.
Equally important is that he *models* this way of pay-
ing attention. He lets his listening be observed. "We
would watch him look up and his face go keen / till
the walls of the world flared, widened." "Keen" is

a wonderful word in this context, suggesting that the father's face is not only focused and but also eager, receptive. We might imagine an expression of steady, heightened concentration, a slight turn and tilt of the head, as he leans into open awareness. The quality of his attention affects not just him or his family but the world itself, for to listen in this way is boundary-dissolving—it makes the world get bigger, more spacious: "the walls of the world flared, widened." "Flared" is another evocative word, suggesting both an opening out and a sudden burst of light, a moment of illumination.

The father's listening is so subtle and capacious that it exerts a lasting effect on the family, the poet in particular: "we still stand / inviting the quiet by turning the face, / waiting for a time when something in the night / will touch us too from that other place." Notice that Stafford says they "invite" not sounds but "the quiet" in which sounds occur, and that they wait not to hear but to be "touched" by something from that "other place." By imitating the father's mindful listening, they make *contact* with the other world that opens to us only when we quiet ourselves to receive it. Stafford was a Quaker, one of "the quiet of the land," and the poem reflects the Quaker practice of silent meetings, where congregants wait for spiritual "leadings" or "promptings" before speaking. Stafford's own writing practice was similarly devotional. Rising early every morning, Stafford would simply wait in silence for a prompting to lead him into the poem.

Like his father, the poet is also keenly attuned to sounds, in this case the sounds of words. The poem he writes is subtly rhymed: *screen, been, keen; wind, widened, stand; face, place.* We might think of these rhymes—some perfect, some slant—as one line listening to another, mirroring its sound and creating an overall sonic coherence in the poem. And because the son brings such respectful attention to his father's listening, the poem has a doubled quality: mindfulness of mindfulness. Just so, if we bring our own mindful attention to the poem, if we listen to the poem as carefully as the father listens to the world and as the son observes the father, we too can participate in this moment of deep awareness: the walls of the poem are widened and we are invited into the poem and into a more spacious sense of our world.

A similar doubling occurs in Denise Levertov's "Aware," as we eavesdrop on the poet's eavesdropping. The British philosopher John Stuart Mill said that poetry is not heard but "overheard." In lyric poems, we often feel that the poet is speaking more to herself than to us; we are simply allowed to listen in to that interior monologue.

Aware

When I found the door
I found the vine leaves
speaking among themselves in abundant
whispers.
      My presence made them
hush their green breath,
embarrassed, the way
humans stand up, buttoning their jackets,
acting as if they were leaving anyway, as if
the conversation had ended
just before you arrived.
             I liked
the glimpse I had, though,
of their obscure
gestures. I liked the sound
of such private voices. Next time
I'll move like cautious sunlight, open
the door by fractions, eavesdrop
peacefully.

Levertov begins by saying, "When I found the door," and we may feel that she is pointing not to a literal door, or not only to a literal door, but to a portal, an opening into a secret world where plants, and perhaps other beings as well, can be overheard speaking to each other. Awareness is the key to that door—the poem is titled "Aware," after all, not "Vine Leaves"—the kind of awareness that pierces the self-created boundaries that seem to separate us from all other beings.

She finds the vine leaves "speaking among them- selves in abundant / whispers," but her presence makes them "hush their green breath." Levertov presents the vine leaves as having not just the power of speech—and it's wonderful that she describes their breath as visible (and green!)—but also recognizable emotional states. The plants are "embarrassed, the way / humans stand up, buttoning their jackets / acting as if they were leaving anyway." This may seem merely fanciful, the stuff of fairy tales, but we might also understand it as a playful way of suggesting that consciousness does not begin and end in the human brain, that we are not the only beings endowed with awareness or the ability to communicate.

The work of evolutionary ecologist Monica Gagliano would seem to confirm Levertov's observation. In her study plant behavior and signaling, Gagliano joins scientific and shamanic methodologies to suggest that plants possess a kind of intelligence, that they can learn, remember, and communicate. We might keep in mind, too, that Levertov was a child of the sixties, deeply involved in the counterculture and antiwar movement. Levertov experimented with LSD, and it may be that the experience she describes in "Aware" was influenced by psychedelics. The poem certainly captures the sense of aliveness and sentience in all things that one feels when under the influence of sacred medicines. Perhaps the awareness of the title refers not just to the human speaker in the poem but to the plants themselves.

But it is her *response* to having startled the vine leaves into silence that is most important. She realizes that to hear more, she must herself become more quiet, more mindful. Instead of doing something to the vine leaves in order to catch their communication—taking them into the lab and wiring them with supersensitive listening devices, for example—she knows that *she* must make the adjustment. Having had this glimpse, she vows next time to "move like cautious sunlight, open / the door by fractions, eavesdrop / peacefully." The significance of this vow can hardly be overstated. To adjust to the reality, and limits, of life as we find it, rather than forcing it to suit our desires, is the difference between peace and violence, humility and arrogance, a sense of oneness and the illusion of separation.

Both "Listening" and "Aware" point to a realm of subtle sounds that exists just beyond the normal range of human hearing, impaired as it is by our habitual mental states of grasping and aversion, impatience and distraction. But they also suggest that if we bring an inner stillness to our listening, if we attune to sound with a gentle, respectful, self-less attention, we too can access that subtle realm. The poems don't say anything about what we might find there, only that there is something to be found. They invite us to see, and hear, for ourselves.

Meditation: Mindfulness of Sounds

Practicing mindfulness of sounds can heighten our appreciation of poetry, just as reading poetry can heighten our attention to sounds.

Choose a place to sit where you'll be exposed to ambient sounds. You might want to sit outside or near an open window, if that's possible. Begin by bringing a kind attention to your body and feel yourself inhabiting this particular place in the universe, feeling your contact with the floor, your seat on the chair or cushion, your hands on your thighs or resting in a mudra. Feel the breath coming in and out of the nostrils, the rise and fall of the belly. And then notice the sound of your breathing. You might notice if your breathing is loud or soft, smooth or choppy, if the in-breath sounds different than the out-breath. Just notice the sound quality of the breath.

After attending to the breath for a time, expand your awareness to include sounds in the room: the hum of appliances, the ticking of a clock, or simply the sound of the room itself. After every scene in a film, audio technicians record the room in silence to capture what they call the "room tone," so that if they have to re-record the dialogue they'll have the right background sound. See if you can attune to the tone of the room you're sitting in.

Now expand your awareness further to sounds beyond the room: traffic sounds, bird calls, sirens, lawn mowers, leaf blowers, people talking in the street, jets passing overhead; pleasant sounds, irritating sounds, neutral sounds; sounds that are near or far away; sounds that are quick and sharp, or sounds that last longer, that shift and change. Just notice sounds as they arise, last for awhile, and disappear.

Now focus your attention on the space between sounds, on the relative silence in which sounds are coming and going. See if you can let your awareness *become* this space, noticing sounds as they pass through you without clinging to them, resisting them, or judging them in any way. After a time, the sense of a separate self "in here" listening to sounds "out there" may fall away; hearing is just happening.

Bring a gentle curiosity to both sounds and the silence around sounds and rest in spacious awareness, open to receive any insights or discoveries that may come to you.

7

MIRROR POEMS
Rexroth, Ammons, Issa, Zagajewski, Frost, Komunyakaa

I

Poems are like mirrors: we see ourselves in them. Just as when we read about a character in a novel facing a moral dilemma and can't help asking ourselves how we would choose, when we read a powerful poem we can't help feeling, to one degree or another, what the poet feels. There is a kind of limbic resonance, or emotional attunement, between poet and reader. When we read deeply, we experience the poem from the inside, as if what's happening in the poem is happening to us; as if we are seeing, thinking, and feeling what the poet is seeing, thinking, and feeling. The best poems make us feel that the poet is describing *our* experience rather than their own. How did they know that *I* felt this way? How did they allow me to see what I already knew but didn't know that I knew? We see ourselves in poems.

Our brains are hard-wired to work this way. Neuroscientists have identified a set of neurons, called mirror neurons, that enable us to map the movements and feelings of others in our own brains. When I observe someone lifting a glass of water, a subset of the same neurons that are firing in her premotor cortex will fire in my own brain. When I see someone smile, my own neurons for smiling light up. I'll flinch if I watch someone else's finger getting pricked. Mirror neurons are thought to provide the physiological basis for empathy, to play an important role in learning by imitation, and to enable us to sense each other's emotional states and intentions—to read each other's minds. (Some neuroscientists believe that autism and related disorders may be caused by mirror neuron deficit). Recent studies also show that mirror neurons light up not just when we see an action performed by someone else but when we read or hear about it as well. This helps explain why we respond to fictional characters in novels as if they were real people, and why we can so strongly feel the emotions expressed in a poem.

Poets may think of themselves, or their creations, as mirrors. In *Hamlet*, Shakespeare wrote that the poet's job is to "hold a mirror up to nature." In his magnificent meditative poem "Corson's Inlet," about a walk along the shifting dunes of the Jersey shore, A. R. Ammons speaks of, and demonstrates, "the overall wandering of mirroring mind." And in many poems, we witness the poet discovering the way one thing mirrors another, finding unity in diversity, seeing the essential likeness between seemingly dissimilar things.

In Buddhist thought, the image of an empty mirror signifies a mind that is untainted, clear-seeing, free of illusion—a mind that "beholds nothing that is not there and the nothing that is," as Wallace Stevens put it in "The Snow Man." The idea of the mirror, and the act of mirroring, is rich with poetic—and Dharmic—implication. Let's look more closely at several poems that reflect these ideas of mirroring.

Kenneth Rexroth was one of the first American poets to seriously engage with Buddhist philosophy and practice, translating the Zen poets of China and Japan and bringing a Zen-like immediacy to his own writing. In "Empty Mirror," he appears to be describing meditation.

Empty Mirror

As long as we are lost
In the world of purpose
We are not free. I sit
In my ten foot square hut.
The birds sing. The bees hum.
The leaves sway. The water
Murmurs over the rocks.
The canyon shuts me in.
If I moved, Basho's frog
Would splash in the pool.
All summer long the gold
Laurel leaves fell through space.
Today I was aware
Of a maple leaf floating
On the pool. In the night
I stare into the fire.
Once I saw fire cities,
Towns, palaces, wars,
Heroic adventures,
In the campfires of youth.
Now I see only fire.
My breath moves quietly.
The stars move overhead.
In the clear darkness

Only a small red glow
Is left in the ashes.
On the table lies a cast
Snake skin and an uncut stone.

Rexroth's simple, declarative sentences capture the *thusness* of the present moment, just what's happening right now. "I sit in my ten foot square hut. / The birds sing. The bees hum. / The leaves sway. The water / murmurs over the rocks." In this kind of bare attention the mind becomes an "empty mirror," not adding to, or making a story about, what it sees. In such a state, the highlight of the day is a moment of empty awareness fully experienced: "Today I was aware / of a maple leaf floating / on the pool."

But when the poet looks back on his youth, he sees the troubling human tendency toward self-aggrandizement, the way we get trapped in our fantasies and projections, the self-centered stories we impose on the world and the violence they so often lead to:

In the night
I stare into the fire.
Once I saw fire cities,

Towns, palaces, wars,
Heroic adventures,
In the campfires of youth.

"Now," the poet says, "I see only fire." Direct perception, nothing added. Having turned away from "the world of purpose," he rests in a stillness in which "inner" and "outer," the vastness of the universe and the intimacy of the breath, mirror each other. "My breath moves quietly. / The stars move overhead." And then the poem closes with a striking image of transformation and wholeness: "On the table lies a cast / snake skin and an uncut stone." The luminous clarity of these objects is the gift that comes when the mind is fully present, free of illusion.

In "Reflective," A. R. Ammons shows us a different kind of mirroring—the sense that when we look at nature, nature is looking back at us.

Reflective

I found a
weed
that had a

mirror in it
and that
mirror

looked in at
a mirror
in

me that
had a
weed in it

Ammons comes out of the tradition of Emerson and
Whitman in American poetry, but was also deeply
influenced by Taoist thought. Like Whitman and
Lao Tzu, he rejected conventional hierarchies of
high and low, important and unimportant. In his
poem "Still," Ammons declares: "Though I have
looked everywhere / I can find nothing lowly / in
the universe." So it is no accident that he finds this
moment of connection not with a flower but with
a weed, something ordinarily regarded as "lowly"
and unwanted. But what is that mirror he finds
there? A drop of water in which he can see himself?
And what is the mirror in him? Is that simply the
mind that mirrors all things when it is clear? Or is
it a simultaneous—mirrored—awareness between

weed and man that is being described? By saying that the weed "looks" at him, Ammons suggests some level of awareness or consciousness in the weed, and implies that the weed is seeing itself in the poet, just as the poet is seeing himself in the weed. But however we make sense of what's happening in the poem is not as important as recognizing the truth of interconnectedness that the poem enacts. The weed is in him and he is in the weed. They are not separate. Nor is their relationship hierarchical; man and weed are on an equal footing, given equal space in the poem. The poem itself is perfectly balanced, it's two parts mirroring each other. The first part, about the mirror in the weed, is six lines containing thirteen words, and the second part, about the mirror in the man, is six lines containing thirteen words. In this way, the poem's form reflects its content.

When we read the poem, even though we know that the poet is describing an experience *he* had, because we hear in our minds that "*I* found a weed," on some level we experience *ourselves* finding that weed, seeing the mirror in it that reflects the mirror in us that has a weed in it. We know the poem from the inside; we look at it, but we are also inside the poem looking at what the poet sees. Just as the poet is in the weed and the weed is in the poet, the poem is in us, and we are in the poem.

Like Ammons, the great Japanese haiku poet Kobayashi Issa was drawn to small things. Many of his poems bring an intimate attention to insects and other creatures typically regarded as subjects too lowly for poetry.

> The distant mountains
> are reflected in the eye
> of the Dragonfly

> —translated from the Japanese by Sam Hamill

Here, Issa reverses the polarity of large and small, framing the vastness of distant mountains within the tiny eye of the dragonfly. What a remarkable thing to notice—and to write a poem about! But the poem also represents the poet's act of seeing; Issa sees the dragonfly and what the dragonfly sees, and also what the dragonfly sees reflected on the surface of its eye. And so the act of seeing is doubled. When we add in our own seeing, the mirroring gets even more layered. The poem might be rewritten in this way:

The distant mountains
are reflected in the eye
of the dragonfly,
which is reflected
in the eye of the poet,
which is reflected
in the eye of the reader.

Issa wisely chooses, as the haiku form demands, not to expand the poem in this way, leaving the reader to discover whatever further connections might be implicit in this simply rendered but complex observation. We might say that the poem is about the variability of perspective, and that it enacts a de-centering of the human point of view, as Issa makes his own seeing secondary to the insect's— an aesthetic choice that is itself full of ethical and philosophical implication. The poem also models a quality of attention that is truly remarkable. How still and attentive would you have to be to see what is reflected in the eye of a dragonfly? And what way of being in the world would you have to practice just to *want* to notice such things? You would have to be willing to forget yourself for a while, to pour yourself entirely into the act of noticing. The poem encourages us to look more closely, more mindfully, at the world, especially at those things typically regarded as insignificant or unworthy of our attention. Who knows what we might find there?

In "Auto Mirror," the Polish poet Adam Zagajewski makes explicit what Issa implies.

Auto Mirror

In the rear-view mirror suddenly
I saw the bulk of the Beauvais Cathedral;
great things dwell in small ones
for a moment.

> —translated from the Polish by Clare Cavanagh
> and Benjamin Ivry

These two poems are remarkably similar. Just as Issa finds distant mountains reflected in the eye of a dragonfly, Zagajewski sees a huge cathedral reflected in his car's rear-view mirror. We feel the looming presence of the medieval church, the weight of its "bulk" held within the tiny frame of the mirror. But unlike Issa, Zagajewski draws a conclusion from this observation: "Great things dwell in small ones / for a moment." This assertion lends itself to a variety of interpretations.

The poem may be describing itself here, demonstrating the truth it asserts: Like the mirror that holds the church, the poem contains a big idea in a small space. Or the poem may be pointing to the way the extraordinary appears within the ordinary, the magical within the mundane, the past within the present. Many other versions of the great in the small might occur to us, but we can't overlook that it's a cathedral and not an office building or a statue that the poet sees in his rearview mirror, and so the poem invites us to consider its spiritual dimension. We might say that the cathedral dwells in the mirror the way the sacred dwells in the profane, or the soul within the body. "Dwells" is a wonderful choice, a word that originally meant *to linger, to be delayed*, but which we now associate with having a home, a dwelling place. The qualifying phrase "for a moment" underscores the temporary nature of all such dwellings, though the moment of recognition, of seeing the large in the small, is given an extended lifespan in the poem itself.

II

Robert Frost's "Tree at My Window" doesn't contain an image of a mirror, but the whole poem suggests a mirroring awareness between the poet and the tree that seems to watch over his sleep.

Tree at My Window

Tree at my window, window tree,
My sash is lowered when night comes on;
But let there never be curtain drawn
Between you and me.

Vague dream-head lifted out of the ground,
And thing next most diffuse to cloud,
Not all your light tongues talking aloud
Could be profound.

But tree, I have seen you taken and tossed,
And if you have seen me when I slept,
You have seen me when I was taken and swept
And all but lost.

That day she put our heads together,
Fate had her imagination about her,
Your head so much concerned with outer,
Mine with inner, weather.

The poem begins with a physical proximity
and a syntactical parallelism, "Tree at my win-
dow, window tree," that already suggests connec-
tion. This mirroring in the opening stanza deepens
when the speaker calls the tree "Vague dream-head
lifted out of the ground." In addressing his poem

to the tree and attributing the power of speech to it—"Not all your light tongues talking aloud / Could be profound"—Frost treats the tree like a sentient being. Doing so may at first seem fanciful or merely an example of poetic license. But what is poetic license other than the freedom to trust our intuitive ways of knowing, our felt sense of the aliveness of the world within and around us that the hyper-rationalist scientific worldview has sought to discredit and dismiss? Frost was strongly influenced by both Ralph Waldo Emerson and the seventeenth century Swedish mystic Emanuel Swedenborg who saw nature and spirit as deeply intermingled. Frost's mother was a devout Swedenborgian and Frost himself was baptized and brought up in the Swedenborgian faith. Frost "heard voices" as a child and was deemed to have "second sight" by his mother. As an adult, he described himself as a mystic. In speaking to and attributing consciousness to the tree, he is not being "poetic" but pointing to the deeper truth of our interconnectedness with all of nature.

We might note here that science is finally catching up with what poets and mystics have known for millenia. Thanks to forest ecologist Suzanne Simard and others, scientific research now shows that trees are remarkably social beings, that they share resources, and that in fact they do communicate with each other, sending chemical and hormonal signals via the mycelium, the vast underground network of fungi that links up a forest root system into a single organism. Perhaps they communicate with us as well.

Like his own dreaming head, the dream-head of the tree sways just beyond his window as he sleeps. And this visual/metaphorical affinity between the speaker and the tree leads to a more significant mirroring:

> But tree, I have seen you taken and tossed,
> And if you have seen me when I slept,
> You have seen me when I was taken and swept
> And all but lost.

Frost's life was filled with loss, early and late, and the anxiety that accompanies such loss. His father died when he was eleven, leaving the family destitute. His sister was mentally unstable and had to be institutionalized, as did his daughter Irma. His son Carol committed suicide. Four of Frost's six children died, two quite young. Frost himself struggled with depression and feared at times for his own sanity. The tossing and turning he describes in the poem comes from intense and prolonged suffering. And yet this act of attunement, seeing and being seen, is comforting. Writing the poem must have afforded some comfort as well. Frost once remarked of the writing process: "There is nothing so composing as composition."

> That day she put our heads together,
> Fate had her imagination about her,
> Your head so much concerned with outer,
> Mine with inner, weather.

In the final stanza, Frost uses a folksy expression in a characteristically subtle way, suggesting both that his head and the tree's head are literally together, on either side of the window, and that they are thinking together, as when we say, "Let's put our heads together and figure this out." The poem's form also expresses the theme of connection. The first three stanzas follow an *a-b-b-a* rhyme scheme, but in the concluding stanza every line ends with the same rhyme sound, a sonic culmination of the mirroring that has occurred throughout the poem. In "Tree at My Window," the boundary between inner and outer has been blurred, if not erased, by

the bond between the wakeful speaker and the wit-
nessing presence of the tree.

Yusef Komunyakaa gives us a much more visually
and emotionally complex kind of mirroring in his
poem about the Vietnam Veterans Memorial in
Washington, D.C.

Facing It

My black face fades,
hiding inside the black granite.
I said I wouldn't,
dammit: No tears.
I'm stone. I'm flesh.
My clouded reflection eyes me
like a bird of prey, the profile of night
slanted against morning. I turn
this way—the stone lets me go.
I turn that way—I'm inside
the Vietnam Veterans Memorial
again, depending on the light
to make a difference.
I go down the 58,022 names,
half-expecting to find
my own in letters like smoke.

I touch the name Andrew Johnson;
I see the booby trap's white flash.
Names shimmer on a woman's blouse
but when she walks away
the names stay on the wall.
Brushstrokes flash, a red bird's
wings cutting across my stare.
The sky. A plane in the sky.
A white vet's image floats
closer to me, then his pale eyes
look through mine. I'm a window.
He's lost his right arm
inside the stone. In the black mirror
a woman's trying to erase names:
No, she's brushing a boy's hair.

Right away, the poem occupies a shifting ground between literal and metaphorical meanings. The title suggests that the speaker is facing the wall of names that is the memorial, but also the grief and trauma of his own war experience. Part of the power of the memorial itself is that we see our own faces in the wall. Our own image merges with the names of those who died, abolishing the sense of separation we might otherwise feel: the war and those who lost their lives in it are over there and we are here, safe and sound. When you look *at* the memorial you are in it, too. The speaker of the poem registers this at the outset: "My black face fades / hiding inside the black granite." His "clouded reflection" looks back at him "like a bird of prey." He is both stone and flesh, both inside and outside the wall, which absorbs rather than keeps out those who look at it. This blurring of the line between outside and inside occurs throughout the poem. "I turn / this way—the stone lets me go. / I turn that way—I'm inside / the Vietnam Veteran's Memorial." "Names shimmer on a woman's blouse / but when she walks away / the names stay on the wall." A white vet "has lost his right arm / inside the wall." And when the speaker touches the name of Andrew Johnson, he re-experiences the shock of the soldier's death, a literal flashback: "I see the booby trap's white flash."

The poem is filled with these powerful, boundary-dissolving images, a mixture of perception and misperception, caused in part by the tears the speaker fails to hold back. But none is more arresting than the final image of the woman who at first appears to be "erasing names," as if by doing so she might bring back the dead who are represented on the "black mirror" of the wall. The speaker then sees what she's really doing and corrects his mistake: "No, she's brushing a boy's hair." Perhaps she is comforting the boy; it may be that the boy's father is represented on that wall. We can't know for sure, but that the poem ends with this instinctive gesture of grooming, and the nurturing it implies, offers an evocative counterpoint to the terrible fruits of violence and war the wall memorializes.

The poem doesn't just describe an experience, it brings us vividly inside it. That's another boundary the poem dissolves: the separation between reader and writer. We see the speaker before the wall but, like the white vet whose "pale eyes look through" the speaker's, we too see through his eyes and are there, both inside and outside the wall, inside and outside the mirror of the poem.

The belief that we are separate from each other and from the world we see "out there," is one of the most difficult illusions to overcome. Mirror poems like those we've been exploring have the power not only to describe the truth of non-separation but to help us—if we read with our full capacity for empathic engagement—to see and *feel* that truth, and to live it.

Meditation: Entering the Poem

Pick one of your favorite poems from *The Poetry of Impermanence, Mindfulness, and Joy* (or from another collection) and place it near your meditation cushion or chair. Take a few moments to become mindful, feeling your feet on the floor, your seat on the cushion or chair, the rise and fall of the breath. Let thoughts and sensations come and go and return to spacious awareness when you find that you've become lost in a story. Rest in the space of this open, receptive, relaxed alertness.

When you feel settled, turn to your poem and read it slowly three or four times, pausing between each reading, and reading the poem aloud the last time. Let yourself savor the sounds and rhythm of the poem, its images, its statements, its twists and turns and moments of beauty or insight. Allow your appreciation to deepen and grow without thinking too much about what the poem means. Give your attention to what's happening within the space of the poem: appealing clusters of sounds, the sudden rightness of a metaphor, the authority or vulnerability of the poem's voice, the way particular words seem to shine with a special resonance.

Now see if you can *enter* the poem. You might imagine that the title (or first line if it has no title) as a kind of gate or threshold, and that once you've opened or crossed it you are no longer outside the poem thinking about it but inside experiencing it. If it's a poem that tells a story or describes an action, let yourself become that speaker and see yourself doing what they do, feeling what they feel, seeing what they see, saying what they say. If the poem is more abstract, a series of statements or images rather than a story or an action, see if you can inhabit those thoughts and images; imagine that *you* are making those statements, creating those images which, in fact, you are, since they come alive only when someone reads them. Or perhaps there is some other way for you to step over the boundary that separates you from the poem. Find what works for you but keep as your goal not more thoughts about the poem but greater intimacy with it.

Now return to a longer meditation, your usual period of time, and without thinking about the poem, notice whatever feeling tone or emotional coloring remains from your experience of reading it. Just allow that residue to be there for however long it persists, and if images or words from the poem come into your awareness, just let them pass through without getting carried away by them. You might also see if any insight arises, if the poem has something more to say to you, something more to reveal.

Let that go and simply rest in awareness until the end of your meditation. Now return to your poem and read it again, noticing if you have a different experience of it after sitting with it in this way.

8

SYMPATHETIC JOY
Chuang Tzu

❧

Some poems present us with competing world views and ask us, explicitly or implicitly, to choose between them. Chuang Tzu's "The Joy of Fishes" is a particularly compelling example of such a poem. It presents a philosophical debate that takes up questions that are very much alive today: Are we locked within our own limited, subjective awareness or deeply connected with all other beings? Is our knowing confined to what can be proved, or does it extend into a mystery we can sense but never fully understand? Do we identify with the rational mind that thrives on logical distinctions or with the open heart that feels its way toward wholeness?

The Joy of Fishes

Chuang Tzu and Hui Tzu
Were crossing Hao river
By the dam.

Chuang said:
"See how free
The fishes leap and dart:
That is their happiness."

Hui replied:
"Since you are not a fish
How do you know
What makes fishes happy?"

Chuang said:
"Since you are not I
How can you possibly know
That I do not know
What makes fishes happy?"

Hui argued:
"If I, not being you,
Cannot know what you know
It follows that you
Not being a fish
Cannot know what they know."

Chuang said:
"Wait a minute!
Let us get back
To the original question.
What you asked me was

'*How do you know*
What makes fishes happy?'
From the terms of your question
You evidently know I know
What makes fishes happy.

"I know the joy of fishes
In the river
Through my own joy, as I go walking
Along the same river."

—translated from the Chinese by
Thomas Merton

Hui Tzu, Chuang Tzu's friend and philosophical foil in "The Joy of Fishes," was a follower of Mohism, a school of thought that prized rationalism and utilitarianism and derided the spontaneous intuitive wisdom of mystics like Lao Tzu and Chuang Tzu. Mohist thought depends on careful definition of terms, the upholding of rigid categories, and strict adherence to logical argumentation. Here, Hui Tzu takes the position that one cannot know what the fishes are feeling simply because there is no logical, empirical basis for that knowing. "Since you are not a fish, / how can you know /

what makes fishes happy?" Taken to its extreme, such a view implies that we are separate from all other creatures, that we can know only what we have directly experienced ourselves, that there is no empathic resonance between the human and non-human worlds.

At first, Chuang Tzu accepts the terms of Hui Tzu's argument and tries to turn it back on him. "Since you are not I, / How can you possibly know / That I do not know / What makes fishes happy?" Hui Tzu seizes upon this rhetorical mistake and seems to trap Chuang Tzu in his own logic: "If I, not being you / Cannot know what you know, / It follows that you / Not being a fish / Cannot know what they know." At which point, Chuang employs a clever bit of sophistry, taking a page from the Mohist playbook by focusing on the *terms* of Hui's question. Because Hui asks *how* Chuang knows, he appears to accept that Chuang *does* know, only questioning the means by which he's arrived at that knowledge.

And that is a question Chuang is happy to answer: "I know the joy of fishes / In the river / Through my own joy as I go walking / Along the same river." Here the poem suddenly reaches a higher emotional register, as Chuang's statement leaps forth, like the fish whose leaping has spawned the argument itself. We, too, may feel a surge of emotion here, an unassailable sense of rightness beyond all argument, at Chuang's assertion of a mirroring emotion between himself and the fishes. The poem moves from heady logic and rhetorical cleverness to a profound statement of embodied truth. It is the bodily resonance with the fishes, the sense of a single emotion being experienced simultaneously by two seemingly separate beings that allows Chuang to *know* the joy of fishes. And so we arrive at a very different way of being and knowing in the world, one that recognizes our basic connectedness with all life and trusts the felt sense of resonance as a reliable indicator of that connectedness.

Interestingly, some marine biologists and wildlife experts suggest that fish often jump out of the water as an expression of "bodily exuberance," which is another way of saying "they jump for joy." They may leap to escape predators or to feed, to rid themselves of parasites or, in the case of salmon, to overcome barriers; but when they leap in the absence of those specific purposes, they are leaping because they can, because it feels good.

But while Chuang wins the argument in the poem, the worldview represented by Hui—the rationalist, materialist, utilitarian worldview—has clearly dominated modern Western culture, and with disastrous results. The horrors we have visited upon the earth and the creatures of the earth result, directly and indirectly, from our illusory sense of separation from the whole, our disconnection and imagined superiority to all other life forms. And so this poem, written more than two thousand years ago, speaks with extraordinary urgency to our own moment of ecological crisis. Or perhaps it would be more true to say our moment of *empathic* crisis, a crisis that asks us to choose: Do we *feel with* all other life forms on the planet, or deny our emotional connection and treat them as commodities or "natural resources" to be exploited or "preserved"? If we *feel with,* if we recognize and cultivate our empathic resonance with life in all its manifestations, then on some fundamental level the crisis can at least be understood within the proper ethical/spiritual framework, and we can begin to heal the self-inflicted wound of separation we are suffering from so acutely right now.

Chuang Tzu's poem invites us to feel with him as he feels with the fish, so that the joy of fishes becomes Chuang Tzu's joy, which in turn becomes our joy, as a single feeling is refracted across time and space through the magical powers of language. To connect with the poem in this way is to reconnect with the whole, and any experience of wholeness, in poetry as in life, is healing.

9

CAUTIONARY TALES
Kay Ryan AND *Ellen Bass*

Poems can help us wake up: from our sensory numbness; from the illusion of separation; from our habitual ways of thinking, feeling, and seeing; from the unconscious belief that we will live forever. We all know, in an abstract way, that we're going to die, but the long habit of living and our aversion to contemplating our own death is so strong that, until the shock of a diagnosis or the death of someone we love, we keep the reality of our existential situation well below the level of conscious awareness. Deliberate practices are needed to pierce our slumber. "Death is real," the Buddha taught. "It comes without warning. This body will be a corpse."

Indeed, in some Buddhist traditions in India and Thailand, monks are instructed to meditate all night at the charnel grounds to observe the ultimate law of impermanence in the decomposition of the body. In the West, a sub-genre of still-life painting, the *memento mori,* reminds us of the fleeting nature of life. These paintings, mostly from the European Renaissance, feature skulls, hourglasses or clocks, flowers, extinguished or guttering candles, blemished fruit, or other objects visibly subject to decay. Or they might portray a feast abruptly departed, the wine goblet tipped over, as if the feaster had been suddenly stuck down. In poetry, too, the brevity of life and unpredictability of death has been a major theme from antiquity to the present day. The persistence and pervasiveness of such spiritual and artistic practices suggest just how difficult it is to wake up—and remain awake—to the truth of our mortality.

Two contemporary poems, "The Niagara River" by Kay Ryan and "If You Knew" by Ellen Bass, vividly explore the tensions between knowing and not-knowing that truth.

The Niagara River

As though
the river were
a floor, we position
our table and chairs
upon it, eat, and
have conversation.

As it moves along,
we notice—as
calmly as though
dining room paintings
were being replaced—
the changing scenes
along the shore. We
do know, we do
know this is the
Niagara River, but
it is hard to remember
what that means.

"The Niagara River" has a parable-like quality about it; the language is ordinary but the situation it describes is clearly symbolic. Like all parables, it uses a simple, evocative story to illustrate a spiritual lesson, to warn us against folly and guide us toward wisdom. In a powerful but impersonal way, the poem dramatizes our obliviousness to the truth of impermanence, the way we mistake flux for stasis, the flow of a river for the stability of a floor. It also points to the way we ignore the change we do see. "We notice—as / calmly as though / dining room paintings / were being replaced— / the changing scenes / along the shore." Ryan uses a

curious analogy, one that distances and aestheti-
cizes the process of unceasing change. The veneer
of civilization—suggested here by dining rooms
and paintings on the walls—is designed in part to
distract us from the fact of our existential vulner-
ability. Change is happening, but that's no reason
to interrupt our pleasant dinner conversation, no
reason to alter the way we live.

But in reflecting on my own inner experi-
ence as I read the poem, I notice that even though
Ryan consistently uses the plural pronoun "we," I
imagine a couple, or a dinner party, floating on
that river—that is, I imagine *other people* heading
blithely toward the falls. I unconsciously exempt
myself from their situation and think: How can
they be so oblivious? How can they forget that
they're floating not just on any river but the *Niag-*
ara River? But in fact they are aware of their situ-
ation, or at least they know the name of the river
they're on. Ryan emphasizes it through repetition.
"We do know, we do / know, that this is the /
Niagara River, but / it is hard to remember / what
that means." It is as if they/we saw a sign saying
"Niagara River," or heard the roar of the falls, and
thought nothing of it, or found some way to keep
it out of awareness. But by focusing on "them"

rather than myself, I commit the very mistake I'm accusing them of: refusing to see that I'm on that river, too.

The poem takes us to the heart of the issue, the challenge of penetrating the mind's automatic defenses, the challenge of not just noticing the river of unceasing change but understanding the *meaning* of that change, remembering where the flow of life will ultimately take us and living every day in the full awareness of that truth. We may also see that this is not merely a personal problem—of realizing impermanence and living according to its laws and limitations—but also a collective problem: the calamity we are surely headed toward if we cannot awaken from our dream of separation and regain a sense of the sacredness of the earth we are destroying. Civilization as we know it is headed toward the falls.

Unlike "The Niagara River," which takes place in the symbolic, impersonal realm of parable, Ellen Bass's "If You Knew," brings the problem of impermanence into the reality of daily life. But it, too, explores the tension between knowing and not-knowing, remembering and forgetting, the truth of our mortality.

If You Knew

What if you knew you'd be the last
to touch someone?
If you were taking tickets, for example,
at the theater, tearing them,
giving back the ragged stubs,
you might take care to touch that palm,
brush your fingertips
along the life line's crease.

When a man pulls his wheeled suitcase
too slowly through the airport, when
the car in front of me doesn't signal,
when the clerk at the pharmacy
won't say *Thank you*, I don't remember
they're going to die.

A friend told me she'd been with her aunt.
They'd just had lunch and the waiter,
a young gay man with plum black eyes,
joked as he served the coffee, kissed
her aunt's powdered cheek when they left.
Then they walked half a block and her aunt
dropped dead on the sidewalk.

How close does the dragon's spume
have to come? How wide does the crack

in heaven have to split?
What would people look like
if we could see them as they are,
soaked in honey, stung and swollen,
reckless, pinned against time?

More than any other poem in *The Poetry of Impermanence, Mindfulness, and Joy,* "If You Knew" has directly influenced how I live my life. After trying to write about the poem for weeks, struggling to explain how it works, I realized that the poem needs no help from me. What it's asking of us is absolutely clear: If you really knew that every single being you encounter could die at any moment, how would you relate to them? How close does the dragon's spume have to come, both personally and collectively, before we wake up to the reality of our predicament? What the poem needs is not explication but application.

Bass gives us powerful examples of the way we move through the world when we're *not* attuned to impermanence: impatient, quick to take offense, unwilling to remember that those who arouse our irritation are, like all of us, going to die. We tend to assume the worst when we have a difficult interaction with a stranger. The guy didn't use his turn signal because he's a jerk who thinks he's above such things as traffic laws. The clerk didn't say "Thank you" because she can't be bothered with the social niceties that smooth our daily interactions. We forget that they're vulnerable to the vicissitudes of life just as we are. Maybe the man moving too slowly in the airport is tired or sick or simply lost in his thoughts. Maybe the guy who cut us off just got fired. Maybe the clerk's mother just died. Maybe the last person *they* interacted with was rude, and they're carrying that anger with them. We don't know their circumstances—the infinite causes and conditions that caused them to behave as they have—but we do know with absolute certainty that they're subject to the laws of impermanence, that they're floating on the Niagara River, right next to us.

And, if we could see them through the facade of invulnerability we present to the world, if we could see them "as they truly are, / soaked in honey, stung and swollen, / reckless, pinned against time," we would see their beauty, the way they glow with an inner sweetness; we would see their woundedness, the way life has stung them again and again; we would see their recklessness, the way they seem almost to invite more pain; and we would see their mortality, the way they are fixed, inescapably, by the terms and conditions of time and change. Seeing all this, we might regard them not with irritation but with compassion, with loving-kindness. We might wish for their happiness, their safety, their ease.

Both "The Niagara River" and "If You Knew" offer forceful reminders of the fragility and preciousness of life. They can help us wake up to the fundamental truth of the human condition. And if we regard these poems as teachers, if we read them not as literary performances but as cautionary tales, we might vow to be more patient and forgiving when we encounter difficult people or situations, knowing that we're all in the same boat, and remembering exactly where that boat is headed.

10

WISDOM *and* COMPASSION
WALT WHITMAN

At the height of the American Civil War, Walt Whitman spent three years visiting wounded and dying soldiers in the hospitals in and around Washington, DC. He would bring them small gifts, whatever they most needed or wanted—a pair of socks, some rice pudding, a shot of brandy—and wrote letters home for those who were unable to write themselves, too weak or in many cases illiterate. Most important, he sat and talked with them, sharing with all who desired it the healing power of his presence. Whitman admired the stoicism with which the soldiers bore their suffering—many of them were as young as fifteen and sixteen, with no friends or family near—and often held vigil until they died. By his own estimate, he visited between eighty to a hundred thousand of the wounded and sick. These visits lasted from an hour or two to all day and night. In critical cases he would sometimes take up quarters in the hospital and keep watch several nights in a row.

Conditions in the overcrowded wards were ghastly—gangrene and other infections killed more soldiers than their injuries—and the long hours Whitman spent there nearly ruined his own health. And yet he considered those three years "the greatest privilege and satisfaction, (with all their feverish excitements and physical deprivations and lamentable sights,) and, of course, the most profound lesson of my life." The compassion he brought to wounded and dying soldiers opened him up to "undream'd-of depths of emotion." Nor did he discriminate between Union and Confederate, or between black and white soldiers. "I can say that in my ministerings I comprehended all, whoever came in my way, northern or southern, and slighted none. . . . I was with many rebel officers and men among our wounded, and gave them always what I had, and tried to cheer them the same as any."

Among the many remarkable aspects of Whitman's wartime service, perhaps most remarkable is this willingness to tend to Confederate as well as Union soldiers, even though his own brother had been wounded at Fredericksburg and would later nearly die of starvation in a Confederate prison. Whitman's compassion made no distinctions, and that generosity of spirit informs one of his great short lyrics about the war, written in 1865, after the fighting had ended.

Reconciliation

Word over all, beautiful as the sky!
Beautiful that war, and all its deeds of carnage,
  must in time be utterly lost;
That the hands of the sisters Death and Night,
  incessantly softly wash again, and ever again,
  this soil'd world:
For my enemy is dead—a man divine as myself
  is dead;
I look where he lies, white-faced and still, in the
  coffin—I draw near;
I bend down, and touch lightly with my lips the
  white face in the coffin.

Whitman places the hoped-for reconciliation between North and South within larger cycles of destruction and purification, where Death and Night are personified as sisters who "incessantly softly wash again, and ever again, this soil'd world." (The repetition of soft *s* sounds reinforces the soothing, restorative quality of the process Whitman describes). He may have been thinking of the women who served as volunteer nurses during the war, the way they would have bathed the soldiers, cleaned their wounds, endlessly it must have seemed. But from witnessing such specific acts of care, Whitman creates an image of cosmic cleansing, a sense that the masculine forces of war and violence will always be met and transformed by the feminine energies of compassion and renewal.

In the second part of the poem, Whitman gives us a specific act of earthly reconciliation, as he bends down and kisses his "enemy" where he lies "white-faced and still, in the coffin." He calls this fallen Confederate solider "my enemy" but recognizes that ultimately he is "divine as myself"; that there is no difference, no separation, between them; that their shared divinity—in Buddhist terms, we might say their basic goodness—is vastly more important, more real, than their allegiance to opposing sides of the conflict. But what an extraordinary thing to say, and to do. Whether or not Whitman actually kissed a Confederate solider in his coffin—it's quite possible he may have done so—or simply imagined it, the gesture, the willingness to make contact, to bridge the physical space between them, represents an act of reverence that transcends all boundaries.

"Reconciliation" embodies the truth of non-separation; we see that truth not only described but acted out before us. As such, the poem models a quality of loving awareness and compassionate behavior we might aspire to ourselves. Can we see the divinity in those we regard as enemies? Can we connect with the basic goodness that exists undisturbed below whatever harmful mind-states we encounter in another? Can we act with gentleness and kindness even in the midst of hatred and violence? No doubt we will often fail, but reading deeply and holding in mind poems like Whitman's "Reconciliation" can help keep the aspiration alive.

While "Reconciliation" gives us an exemplary mode of behavior, a moment of transcendent compassion, another poem, "When I Heard the Learn'd Astronomer," dramatizes an exemplary mode of awareness, a moment of boundary-dissolving oneness with the cosmos. Here, Whitman describes a lecture on astronomy that leaves him weary.

> When I heard the learn'd astronomer,
> When the proofs, the figures, were ranged in
> columns before me,

When I was shown the charts and diagrams, to
    add, divide, and measure them,
When I sitting heard the astronomer where he
    lectured with much applause
      in the lecture-room,
How soon unaccountable I became tired
    and sick,
Till rising and gliding out I wander'd off by myself,
In the mystical moist night-air, and from time
    to time,
Look'd up in perfect silence at the stars.

We might begin by noticing the poem's form: a single sentence stretching over eight lines that fall naturally into two four-line sections. The first four lines all begin in the same way, an initial repetition—the technical term is *anaphora*—that Whitman frequently uses in his poems. "When I heard . . . When the proofs . . . When I was shown . . . When I sitting heard . . ." The sentence builds tension by giving us four dependent clauses before delivering the main clause: "How soon unaccountable I became tired and sick . . ." ("Unaccountable" is wonderfully ironic here, as Whitman undermines the lecturer's language of counting and accounting by showing its limitations, what it can't account for, the life of our emotions). And so we feel the poet's growing frustration as he sits in the lecture room listening to a soul-deadening analysis of the starry sky.[1] This frustration, and its release, is perfectly enacted in the second part of the poem, as the final four lines take on a smoother, lighter rhythm and softer sounds. The sense of the poem, but also its sound, create a palpable feeling of freedom and expansiveness as the poet trades the confinement of the lecture hall, with its heady analysis and loud applause, for solitary wandering and perfect silence: "Till rising and gliding out I wandered off by myself / in the mystical moist night air and from time to time, / look'd up in perfect silence at the stars."

But more than a critique of a particular lecture, the poem rejects a way of understanding the world that is devoid of wonder and reverence and relies exclusively on reductive forms of reasoning: proofs and figures, charts and diagrams. Such a method both arises from and solidifies our illusory sense of separation from the whole. The human observer is here and "nature"—whether stars or forests or oceans or the earth itself and all its nonhuman life forms—is "out there," as if we are not part of nature and can therefore do whatever we want to it.

---

1 Some art historians surmise that Van Gogh's famous painting *Starry Night* was inspired by Whitman's poetry, which the painter greatly admired.

The spiritual exhaustion Whitman feels in the face of such thinking is becoming widespread in modern societies, as each technological advance takes us further from our true home—the actual earth, our physical reality—which our virtual realities increasingly obscure. The noise, disconnection, and accelerating activity of contemporary culture make it harder and harder to experience moments of quiet mystery such as Whitman describes. And yet the poem is a reminder that we are free to get up and walk out—of the story we're telling ourselves, or that the culture is telling us, about reality; that we can reject the materialist way of comprehending the world and choose to embrace the whole with wonder and respect, as Whitman does here.

In both his life and his writing, Whitman presents an exemplary figure. His wartime service represents an act of sustained compassion unsurpassed in the lives of American writers. And in his poems, there are moments of profound empathic connection, like the one in "Reconciliation," and of spacious awareness, like the one in "When I Heard the Learn'd Astronomer," that can inspire us to bring the better angels of our own nature, our Buddha nature, more fully into the world.

Meditation: Sit Like a Tree

It is no surprise that the Buddha attained liberation under a tree. He had been practicing in the forests of India for many years, surrounded by trees. Earlier, he had reached a crucial turning point in his awakening while sitting under a rose apple tree, when he recalled a childhood experience of natural ease and happiness and realized he must reject the extreme asceticism that had nearly killed him. If we're able to do our sitting practice outside, under or near trees, we may feel a continuity with the Buddha's forest practice and take strength from the steadiness and composure of trees.

This meditation is best done in a forest or park setting, but if neither is available to you, simply find a quiet place to sit outside where you're not likely to be disturbed. After you take your seat, make the intention to sit like a tree. You might imagine the bones of your feet as roots that reach down into the ground and spread out around you, drawing up deep earth energies into your limbs. Imagine your torso like a tree trunk, solid but flexible, moving nutrients throughout your body while you're breathing in and out.

Sit with the imperturbable presence of a tree that has lived for hundreds of years, weathering storms and droughts without complaint. Allow thoughts, sounds, sensations, emotions to come and go like clouds or birds or breezes while you remain steadfast in awareness, unmoving in the midst of it all.

You might imagine that the other trees around you are your sangha and let their calm presence support your practice, all of you breathing together, feeling the same sun, the same breeze, hearing the same sounds, rooted in the same earth. If no trees are nearby, you might imagine that you're sitting in a forest or under a tree that has been particularly important to you, perhaps a tree from your childhood. Or you might hold in mind the image of an archetypal tree, the Bodhi tree, or the tree of life, or a mother tree.[2]

Rest in awareness, feeling your connection to earth and sky, and when you feel pulled away by thoughts and emotions, gently return to the steadfastness of a tree and trust that you can withstand whatever storms may come.

---

2 Forest Ecologist Suzanne Simard has identified mother trees, the largest trees in forests that act as central hubs for vast below-ground mycorrhizal networks. A mother tree supports seedlings by infecting them with fungi and supplying them the nutrients they need to grow.

Part
Two

HOW *to* LEAD *a* DHARMA *and* POETRY DISCUSSION

As a poet and meditator, I always lean in when I hear a poem read during a Dharma talk. And in my twenty years of mediation practice, it seems that poems are appearing more frequently in Buddhist teachings. But these poems are almost always offered simply to illustrate a point, never for their intrinsic value or as vehicles for exploring the Dharma. Or if they are more fully explored, it's often in the form of over-meticulous line-by-line explications of ancient sutras or didactic poems like Shantideva's *Way of the Bodhisattva.* On one level, this makes sense: Dharma talks follow certain conventions that don't easily allow for going more deeply into a poem. And because Dharma teachers usually aren't poets themselves, or teachers of poetry, they may feel unsure about how to explore a poem in depth, or lead a discussion about poetry. This limited use of poetry is understandable, but it misses a wonderful opportunity for deepening our understanding of the Buddha's teachings.

One of the most enjoyable aspects of poetry discussions is that they can engage the whole group in a way that passively listening to a talk cannot, giving participants an opportunity to share their insights and personal experience, and to have those insights and experiences received and considered. Many community members have decades of Dharma practice under their belts, and yet they are rarely given space to share what they've learned. Poetry discussions take full advantage of the collective wisdom and experience of the group and can be a remarkable bonding experience for sangha members.

It can be challenging, though, to lead a successful poetry discussion, one that doesn't lapse into awkward silence or get bogged down in competing interpretations and heady analysis. Over the course of many years of teaching I've found a simple method of leading discussions that rarely fails to elicit lively engagement and that often leads to profound insights. I begin by reading the poem aloud, or having a sangha member read it, so that everyone has a fresh—and shared—experience of the poem. If it's a short poem, I may read it a second time. After allowing for some silence to let the poem resonate, I simply invite participants to drop the impulse to analyze and interpret, and instead enter the poem through the doorway of noticing and appreciating, to go straight to what they *enjoy* about a poem.

Instead of focusing on what the poem "means," or what the poet "is saying," which tends to reduce the poem to its paraphrasable content, I'll ask: "What do you notice and appreciate about the poem? What feels lit up for you? What do you *like* about the poem?" Anyone can notice and appreciate. It requires no literary training; indeed, literary training is often an obstacle, as concepts and interpretive strategies can obscure the immediacy of our connection with a poem.

Meditation, on the other hand, is excellent preparation for reading and discussing poetry in this way. Having the poetry discussion after a period of sitting meditation (even if brief) is extremely helpful, as the group will already be in a state of heightened receptivity and awareness. The kind of attention we bring to meditation—alert, open, curious, mindful—serves us well when we're reading and talking about a poem, just as noticing and appreciating what's happening in a poem supports the bare attention we cultivate in meditation practice. And for the teacher, gently leading students back to noticing and appreciating, if they stray into strained analysis and interpretation, is much like the practice of noting thoughts and coming back to direct experience in meditation.

Asking students what they notice and like about a poem also frees them from feeling that they have to say something smart or offer an interpretation. It takes them *into* the poem, into their own experience of it, rather than separating them from the poem, as analysis and interpretation tend to do. Such an approach elevates enjoyment over understanding. It calls forth enthusiasm rather than anxiety about whether they're "getting it" or not. And such enthusiasm is contagious. It sparks others to say what *they* like, or to reinforce what someone else has said. Poems begin to glow under such collective appreciation. They come alive and offer up their magic more willingly when they're appreciated than when people are arguing over what they might mean, or laying them out for analysis.

It's difficult to resist the figuring-it-out mode, but that way of reading treats poems as little more than frustratingly elusive machines for delivering meaning, where the goal of reading a poem is not to experience it, not to enjoy it, or feel what it makes you feel, but to interrogate it until it coughs up a confession of the secret it has worked so hard to conceal. Such an approach robs poems of their aliveness and, paradoxically, makes our experience of them *less* meaningful rather than more so.

So entering through the doorway of noticing and appreciating is essential. I've also found that echoing or amplifying participants' comments can be quite helpful. Doing so lets them know that you're hearing what they say, considering it, taking it in. Responding to what someone offers, sharing their appreciation ("I love that passage, too!"), or following up on their appreciation ("I'm glad you noticed that the poem uses very short lines—how does that affect the way you experience it?") shows that you value what has been offered and want to build on it. That gives everyone confidence to speak and energizes the group. In such an environment, people are eager to share, eager to connect with the poem, and through the poem with each other and with the teacher. Gone is the anxiety of English class, where fear of sounding foolish, or the need to be right, or the desire to show what you know, often dominates discussion. In its place is the joy of a free-flowing, shared experience.

But poems, like the ones in *The Poetry of Impermanence, Mindfulness, and Joy,* offer more than an opportunity for a pleasurable shared experience, though they do offer that. I've found that they express and embody the Dharma in ways that make them excellent vehicles for teaching. Discussions can be organized around poems in that book's three sections: Impermanence, Mindfulness, and Joy. But within those broad categories, more specific aspects of Buddhist teachings can be illuminated with these poems: non-harming, awareness of awareness, right speech, right action, right mindfulness, clear-seeing, reverence and humility, non-separation, no-self, etc. I don't mean to imply that only poems in my anthology can serve this purpose. The realm of poetry is incredibly rich and varied, and I would encourage anyone who is interested to follow their inclinations and explore whatever poems work best for them. A list of poetry resources—anthologies, websites, etc.—is provided in the Poetry Resources at the end of this book.

Dharma talks are powerful vehicles for delivering the Buddha's teachings; they continue a tradition that goes all the way back to the Buddha himself. But they are inherently hierarchical. The teacher talks and the sangha listens, which is the same basic format as the university lecture. Lectures can be brilliant, entertaining, moving, inspiring, but they do put students in a largely passive role. Listening well can be a deep practice of attention and respect, but more opportunities for group members to actively engage with the teachings in Dharma settings would surely be a welcome innovation. Dharma talks are often followed by a period for questions and answers, but here, too, the hierarchical assumption prevails: the students have the questions and the teachers have the answers.

In mindful poetry discussions, knowledge, insight, wisdom, and enjoyment arise from the group as a whole. (I've found that poetry discussions work best in groups of ten to fifteen participants. If your sangha is larger, senior members can be asked to lead discussions in small groups.) The facilitator guides the discussion—and careful guidance is crucial—but always with the intention of creating and holding a space where all can contribute. Facilitators may have particular insights and perspectives to offer, but these are not placed above the insights of anyone else in the group. Their job is to receive, value, and amplify comments shared by group members; to make sure that no one person dominates; to keep the discussion moving at an appropriate pace (I find that 10–20 minutes on each poem works best, depending on the interest and energy of the group); and to shift the discussion back to noticing and appreciating if it gets bogged down in interpretive arguments or confusions.

For example, it sometimes happens that a participant, instead of focusing on what they like about a poem, will do just the opposite and voice a complaint or confusion: "I don't understand what this line means," or "Why does the poet say _____?" Or they may ignore what's happening on the page and offer what can feel like a forced or fanciful interpretation (of the poem's "hidden" meaning) for which there is no support in the poem itself: "I think this poem about a blackbird is really about World War II." When that happens, note that you hear the participant's concern or interpretation, and gently ask them to return to noticing and appreciating. You might add that critical/interpretive approaches are not without value, but that they don't fit with the purpose and intention of *this* kind of discussion. You might also suggest that when we approach poems through noticing and appreciating we're practicing a form of loving awareness rather than literary analysis. We are practicing being with the poem as it is, rather than demanding that it be what we think it *should* be or that it confess to us what it really means. If we don't immediately or fully understand the poem, we can learn to be OK with that not-knowing and simply enjoy what we do understand. The great English poet John Keats admired this ability "to be in the midst of doubts and mysteries without the irritable reaching after fact and reason."

After the group has spent time noticing and appreciating what's happening in a poem, the discussion can move to what the poems have to teach us about the Dharma, how they reflect and illuminate our own experience of impermanence, suffering, grief, joy, spaciousness, connection, freedom, and the like. Instead of making specific suggestions here about how you might handle this aspect of the discussion, I'll simply point to the essays in this book as examples of how one might explore the Dharma in poetry, and encourage you to trust your own experience and instincts as well as the instincts and experience of the group.

It's important to remember that the Dharma refers not only to the Buddha's teachings as such but also to the truth of things, universal law, the way things are. No special expertise is required to talk about the basic conditions of our human existence, just attention, openness, curiosity, compassion—traits we all share and which poetry both elicits and rewards.

One of the joys (and potential anxieties) of leading a poetry discussion is that you can never predict quite how or where it will go, how the group will respond, or what insights will emerge. It can be scary, but it's also a wonderful opportunity for teachers to practice letting go of expectations and accepting whatever arises. A poetry discussion is wide-ranging, full of wonders, surprises, disappointments, like life itself. Holding space for this aliveness is much more important than whatever might be said during the discussion.

I've found that having that intention and stating it to oneself before the discussion begins can be useful. Before I teach, I say a kind of prayer: *May I be mindful, may I be clear, may I be helpful, may I be open and receptive to whatever arises, and may this be a wonderful experience for all concerned.* I also say a prayer for the participants: *May they be open, receptive, engaged, curious, responsive. May they be peaceful, mindful, happy.* I've found that saying this prayer gives me confidence that I can be a conduit for a fruitful discussion. It eases whatever self-consciousness and performance anxiety I might be feeling and puts the emphasis on making the discussion interesting and helpful for the group. I often emerge from these discussions of poems I've known and taught for years with a new and deeper understanding, and because it follows the aliveness of the group rather than a set goal or pre-determined interpretation, each discussion is fresh and unique, unpredictable and unrepeatable.

I encourage you to enter the experience with a sense of openness, adventure, and generosity.

You never know what may come of it!

WRITING PROMPTS

Even if you don't think of yourself as a writer, you may enjoy the following writing prompts. They invite you to engage creatively with some of the ideas we've been exploring in this book.

Writing Prompt 1:
Making Friends with "Ordinary" Objects

Start with a few minutes of meditation and then bring your attention to something that exists within your daily field of vision, or which you use daily but which you never really pay attention to, something that feels neutral—the lamp on your desk, a doorknob, a coffee cup, a bookcase, etc. Set a timer and focus on that object for two full minutes.

Notice its form and shape, its coloring, its texture, the way it catches light and shadow, the way it stands forth in space—try to take in as much detail as you can. Notice, too, its qualities: is it warm or cool, rounded or flat, simple or complex?

Notice if it seems to have a particular demeanor or personality: open or secretive, inviting or aloof.

Then let your mind simply rest on and with the object, try to experience it as a friend and fellow traveler in this strange journey of life, both of you briefly inhabiting the realm of manifest form before passing on.

Feel yourself breathing and imagine that the object is aware of your presence and your steady gaze.

Be with the object in this way, without agenda or expectation, and when the timer pings, spend another five minutes simply writing whatever comes to you.

Your writing may take the form of a poem or a prose paragraph.

Maybe you imagine a story about the secret lives of lamps, what happens to them when they're turned off while you sleep, what they dream of, how they feel about their use and purpose. Maybe you simply write down the wealth of details that you've observed. Or focus on the warm feeling that has arisen, the new sense of connection you feel with whatever it is you've been looking at. Maybe you imagine what that object would say if it could speak. Simply open to whatever wants to come forth and write with ease, without ambition or goal but to see what the object has communicated to you.

After you've finished writing, bow to the object and thank it for allowing you to be with it in this way.

You may find you've made a new friend.

Writing Prompt 2:
Accepting What Comes

Finding a way to begin is often the hardest part of writing a poem. This exercise, developed by the poet Andrea Hollander, solves that problem by giving you a first line and letting you take it from there.

Begin by becoming mindful, and then open *The Poetry of Impermanence, Mindfulness, and Joy* (or another collection of poems) at random and copy the first line of the poem you've turned to. Close the book without reading the rest of the poem and, without thinking or planning, write down the first thing that comes to mind.

Don't worry about writing something mean-ingful or graceful, just accept whatever comes to you without judging it good or bad. Let one word or line or image suggest the next and allow the momentum of your writing to carry you onward.

Write quickly and don't edit or change anything or try to shape the poem in any particular way.

See if you can let go and simply witness what's coming forth as if someone else were writing it, just as in meditation we notice the contents of our awareness, the thoughts, sensations, stories, feelings, etc., that arise and pass away without our summoning them or controlling them.

Don't censor yourself in any way. Say something outlandish or nonsensical if it occurs to you. Just keep writing.

And when you feel you're finished, pause and look up from your notebook or computer and write a few lines about the first thing you see, either outside or in the room. You might simply write, "And now I notice the wind in the trees or the light on the fire escape or the sound of a siren in the distance." See if this can bring some new energy to your writing, or perhaps suggest a way to end.

When you're done, read what you've written and notice if any moments feel particularly juicy, or if there's more to be said, something else to be explored or elaborated.

Write more, or revise, if the spirit moves you, or simply let what you've written stand as an unfiltered moment of consciousness faithfully recorded, a transcript of the mind moving in language, witnessed but not controlled.

Writing Prompt 3:
Seeing from a Nonhuman Perspective

One of the gifts of poetry is that it can release us from our constricted sense of self and help us feel in communion with a world that is alive, awake and aware. This writing exercise invites us to inhabit other life forms and to see the human world from a nonhuman perspective.

Reread the poems by Issa, "I'm going to roll over" (p. vii), Levertov, "Aware" (p. 61), and Frost, "Tree at My Window" (p. 79), and work with one of the following prompts.

- Imagine how the cricket might respond to Issa, after the poet announces that he's going to roll over and says, "so please move, / cricket."
- Write a dialogue of what the vine leaves were talking about before Levertov's interruption makes them "hush their green breath."
- Imagine what the tree might be thinking or feeling as it watches Frost being "taken and swept and all but lost" in his troubled sleep.

You might begin by sitting in meditation and letting yourself feel what it would be like to let go of your human form.

Trust your imagination to guide you.

The myths of many indigenous peoples look back to an age when humans could shape shift into other animals and communicate with all living things. Trust that access to such transformation and communication is still present deep within your psyche and write whatever comes to you without worrying whether it sounds childish or implausible.

Let yourself be playful. Put yourself in the situation the poem describes and see it from the nonhuman point of view.

Experiment, take risks, say things you didn't know you knew how to say.

When you're done writing, spend some time enjoying your life as a cricket or vine leaf or tree before resuming your human incarnation.

Perhaps you'll feel more open and expansive, more caring and connected, for having taken this journey into the nonhuman realm.

Writing Prompt 4:
Dissolving the Sense of a Separate Self

Many of the poems we've been exploring describe boundary-dissolving experiences, those moments when the feeling of separation falls away and we sense our fundamental oneness with all life. This writing prompt invites you to explore one of your own boundary-dissolving experiences.

Begin with a few minutes of mindfulness practice and then reflect back over your life and see if a moment emerges when you felt the boundaries between you and the world around you relax. Such moments often occur in nature, in meditation, in the unselfconscious flow of movement in dance or sports, in lovemaking, or under the influence of sacred medicines.

They can also happen quite spontaneously in the most unlikely situations. Just allow yourself to recall if you've ever had even a taste of such a moment. And if nothing comes to mind, let yourself imagine what it might feel like to step beyond the sense of being a separate self, to let the anxieties and strivings of the ego dissolve.

Once you have visualized such a moment, notice how it feels in your body to relive it. Let yourself savor it fully before you begin writing, noticing whatever you can remember of the time and place where it happened: the setting, the light, any sounds or prominent sensations, your own presence within the scene, anyone else who was there.

When that becomes clear, begin writing.

You may want to write a narrative about the memory or just put down images and fragments that evoke the experience, trusting that you can organize, develop, and polish it later if you wish.

The main thing is to try to be *in* the experience again as you write, to feel it as fully as possible. Resist the urge to explain it or comment on it and focus instead on recalling it and evoking it as vividly as possible.

After you're done writing, let the words go and return to meditation.

Notice whatever emotions and sensations are most present after having written about your boundary-dissolving experience. Perhaps you'll feel a softening or blurring once again of the lines that seem to separate you from the world.

Writing Promp 5:
The Sacred Pause

Reread "The Sacred Pause" essay in this book and reflect on a time when you were able to drop your habitual patterns and experience a moment of what Ajahn Buddhadasa calls "temporary nirvana."

Start with a brief period of meditation, and then recall a moment when you were able to stop—when you didn't lash out in anger, or withdraw into hurt or judgment or distraction, or when you were able to step away from harried doing and enjoy a moment of pure being.

If you haven't had this kind of experience, imagine a situation where you wish you *had* been able to pause and explore how differently the moment might have played out.

Let yourself fully inhabit this experience.

What were the circumstances that led up to it? How did it feel to have that moment of freedom? What were the consequences—for yourself and for others—of not acting or reacting as you typically do? What did this moment teach you?

After reflecting on this experience, begin to write about it.

You may want to write a prose response to the questions above and shape it into a poem later. Just allow whatever thoughts and feelings associated with this experience of pausing come forth.

As you're writing, pause from time to time and let there be some space before you set down the next line or sentence.

Become mindful, tune into the breath, feel whatever body sensations are most present, and see what wants to arise, what needs your attention, what wants to be said.

Maintain this rhythm of pausing and writing, and let the process be one of allowing and arising rather than planning and doing. In this way, you can practice pausing even as you're writing about it.

Notice how it feels to write in this way, how it's different from your usual way of writing and thinking, and enjoy the quiet, creative spaciousness that may emerge.

EPILOGUE

Russell Delman, an Embodied Life teacher steeped in Feldenkrais and Zen, will often say after a talk or an especially lively discussion: "We've just had a lot of words. Let's pause, let the words go, and return to our direct experience of this present moment." I'd like to apply this suggestion to how you might continue your journey with poetry.

I've given you a lot of words *about* poems, and writing about poetry is a finger pointing at the moon, not the moon itself. Please remember the most important thing is not what you think about a poem—or what a teacher or anyone else says about it—but how you experience it: what you see, feel, remember, imagine. When you enter a poem, you enter an incredibly rich space of interactive awareness. We want to be fully *in* that space of intimate connection, the shared vulnerability of that openness and contact, the mysterious alchemy that can occur when we bring our awareness into the field of awareness the poem has created. Formulating an interpretation of the poem, a statement of what it means, will take you out of that space. Noticing, appreciating, listening, feeling what the poem is showing you will keep you in it.

Nothing could be more important or more urgent right now than to realize the truth of interdependence, the common destiny we share with all life. Bringing poetry more wholeheartedly into our spiritual practice is one of the most powerful ways of knowing and feeling that truth. So find the poems you love, read and reread them, enter them, live in them awhile, and bow to the wisdom you find there.

ACKNOWLEDGMENTS

I'm deeply grateful to Daniel Aitken, Ben Gleason, Kestrel Montague, and the whole team at Wisdom Publications for believing in *The Dharma of Poetry* and bringing it so beautifully to fruition. I'm especially grateful to Josh Bartok, who offered the perfect balance of a sharp eye and a light touch in the editing of this book.

My thanks to Heather Sellers, whose many insights and helpful suggestions greatly improved the final version of this book. Thanks also to Fred Muratori, Chuck Moshontz, Justin Rigamonti, Ken Pallack, and Andrea Hollander for reading individual essays and offering invaluable support and enthusiasm along the way.

Writing *The Dharma of Poetry* would not have been possible without the love and support of my wife, Alice Boyd, who has been intimately involved in all aspects of this book from gestation to completion and who teaches me something new every day about the Dharma of relationship.

Finally, I want to thank all those readers who have responded so powerfully to *The Poetry of*

Impermanence, Mindfulness, and Joy. This book is for everyone, but it is especially for you.

POETRY RESOURCES

ANTHOLOGIES

The Poetry of Impermanence, Mindfulness, and Joy, edited by John Brehm

Poetry of Presence: An Anthology of Mindfulness Poems, edited by Phyllis Cole-Dai and Ruby R. Wilson

The Essential Haiku: Versions of Basho, Buson, & Issa, edited by Robert Hass

Mountain Home: The Wilderness Poetry of Ancient China, edited by David Hinton

Women in Praise of the Sacred: 43 Centuries of Spiritual Poetry by Women, edited by Jane Hirshfield

A Book of Luminous Things: An International Anthology of Poetry, edited by Czeslaw Milosz

The Enlightened Heart: An Anthology of Sacred Poetry, edited by Stephen Mitchell

American Journal: Fifty Poems for Our Time, edited by Tracy K. Smith

Zen Poems of China and Japan: The Crane's Bill, edited by Lucien Stryk and Takaski Ikemoto

The Art of Losing: Poems of Grief and Healing, edited by Kevin Young

WEBSITES

The Academy of American Poets, www.poets.org
Poetry Daily, www.poems.com
The Poetry Foundation, www.poetryfoundation.org

CREDITS

INDEX

A

acceptance
  Accepting What Comes
    writing prompt, 136–37
  challenges of, in Ryan's
    "The Niagara River,"
    102–3
  of impermanence, mortal-
    ity, 99–103
  of not knowing, 129
The Aeneid (Virgil), 3
Ajahn Chah, 23
Ammons, A.R.
  "Corson's Inlet," 69
  "Reflective," 72–75
  "Still," 73
attention, mindful aware-
    ness. *See also* knowing
  achieving through deep
    listening, 59
  and appreciation, grati-
    tude, 27, 125
  in "Aware," 62–63

in "A Cold Spring," 37–38,
    41
in "The distant moun-
    tains," 76
enhancing through poetry,
    xiv, 4
and entering a poem, ix,
    60, 87
as an expression of love, 46
in "Filling Station," 44–45
in "Listening," 58–59
mindful poetry discus-
    sions, 127
in "The old man . . .," 31
and paying attention, 31
poetry as, viii–ix
and seeing interconnec-
    tions, 71–74, 76–77
and silence, 63–64
timelessness of, 49
Auden, W. H., "September,
    1939," 1, xii–xiii
"Auto Mirror" (Zagajewski),
    77–78

155

ABOUT *the* AUTHOR

 **JOHN BREHM** is the author of three books of poetry, *Sea of Faith, Help Is on the Way,* and *No Day at the Beach*. His poems have appeared widely in journals and anthologies, including *Poetry, The Sun, The Gettysburg Review, The Writer's Almanac, Plume, Best American Poetry, The Norton Introduction to Literature*, and many others. He is the editor of *The Poetry of Impermanence, Mindfulness, and Joy* and the associate editor of *The Oxford Book of American Poetry.* He lives in Portland, Oregon, and teaches poetry classes in Portland and in Denver, Colorado. With his wife, Feldenkrais teacher Alice Boyd, he leads mindfulness retreats that incorporate Feldenkrais Awareness through Movement Lessons, meditation, and mindful poetry discussions. He can be found online at johnbrehmpoet.com.

WHAT TO READ NEXT
FROM WISDOM PUBLICATIONS

Poetry of Impermanence, Mindfulness, and Joy
Edited by John Brehm

"This collection would make a lovely gift for a poetry-loving or Dharma-practicing friend; it could also serve as a wonderful gateway to either topic for the uninitiated." —*Tricycle: The Buddhist Review*

Zen Master Poems
Dick Allen

"*Zen Master Poems* features reflection, meditation, mystery, humor, admonition, koans, calm observation, and Buddhist thought for readers and seekers on every path." —*Lion's Roar*

The Wisdom of Listening
Edited by Mark Brady

"This collection of essays raises listening to a spiritual art." —*Sacred Pathways*

About Wisdom Publications

Wisdom Publications is the leading publisher of classic and contemporary Buddhist books and practical works on mindfulness. To learn more about us or to explore our other books, please visit our website at wisdomexperience.org or contact us at the address below.

Wisdom Publications
199 Elm Street
Somerville, MA 02144 USA

We are a 501(c)(3) organization, and donations in support of our mission are tax deductible.

Wisdom Publications is affiliated with the Foundation for the Preservation of the Mahayana Tradition (FPMT).